Complete Living Trust Blueprint

Stress-Free 90-Day Plan
Avoid Probate, Reduce Taxes &
Maximize What You Leave Behind

Ellis Whitmore

Sage Lifestyle Press

Complete Living Trust Blueprint
Stress-Free 90-Day Plan Avoid Probate, Reduce Taxes, & Maximize What You Leave Behind

Published by Sage Lifestyle Press

IMPORTANT LEGAL DISCLAIMER

This book is for educational and informational purposes only and is not intended as legal advice.

The information contained in this book is not a substitute for professional legal counsel. Estate planning laws vary significantly by state and are subject to frequent changes. While the author has made every effort to provide accurate and current information, laws, regulations, and court interpretations may have changed since publication.

The author and publisher specifically disclaim any liability, loss, or risk incurred as a consequence of the use and application of any of the contents of this book. Neither the author nor the publisher is engaged in rendering legal, accounting, or other professional services through this book. If legal advice or other expert assistance is required, the services of a competent professional should be sought.

Individual results may vary. The effectiveness of any estate planning strategy depends on your specific circumstances, state laws, federal tax regulations, and other factors that may change.

No Attorney-Client Relationship. Reading this book does not create an attorney-client relationship between you and the author or publisher. Any information you may send to the author or publisher will not be treated as confidential or privileged.

State Law Variations. Estate planning laws vary significantly from state to state. Examples and strategies discussed in this book may not be applicable or advantageous in your state. Always verify that any strategy is appropriate under your state's current laws.

Tax Considerations. Tax laws are complex and subject to frequent changes. You should consult with a qualified tax professional before implementing any tax-related strategies discussed in this book.

By reading this book, you acknowledge that you understand these limitations and agree to seek appropriate professional advice for your specific situation.

Contents

Introduction

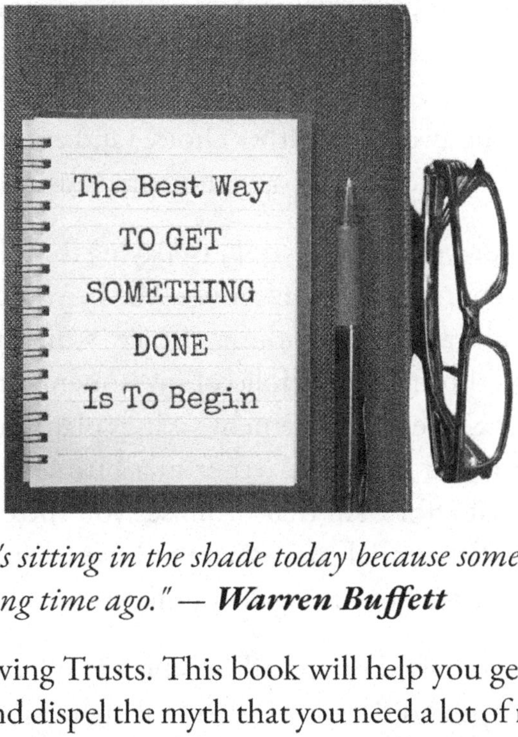

"Someone's sitting in the shade today because someone planted a tree a long time ago." — ***Warren Buffett***

Welcome to Living Trusts. This book will help you get started with the planning and dispel the myth that you need a lot of money before you put these important processes and documents in place. This book helps you decide whether to hire a lawyer or Do-It-Yourself ("DIY"). While the authors have tried to make this technical information easy to read and follow-the nature of the topic is a little thick. We hope that the 90-Day Roadmap will help with the implementation. Congratulations on taking this step to protect your legacy.

Whether you decide you can plan on your own or should hire an attorney, it is important to understand what is involved before you get the ball rolling so that you can ensure you know what you want and what you will be getting. Nothing is worse than spending several thousand dollars not to understand what you received, or not to have it be exactly what you intended. This book helps you **do your homework first**. You will learn what is involved in creating a living trust and perhaps a fuller estate plan.

To create a trust and protect your legacy fully, you need to learn all you can, assess where you are, and decide if you want to use an attorney from the start, or one of the available online applications that exist today. Just be aware that either choice (and even a combination of the two) requires a lot of introspection, preparation, and planning.

You've spent your working years not just paying the bills, but creating abundance for yourself and your family. Maybe you bought a home or condo, bought a certain amount of nice 'stuff', as well as built up cash reserves through a portfolio of investments. You may have a 401k or other tax-deferred retirement savings plans, such as an IRA. Maybe you founded or are a partner in a business, and you reap the profits of that effort. All that promises you future comfort and security. Some of that might allow you to leave a legacy. A trust can help you secure those benefits against unforeseen events.

Many of you have raised or are still raising a family, and manage all the emotional ups and downs of getting it right for everyone. And family is another reason to do this planning today: You are perhaps still raising minor children. What happens if you are gone and are no longer providing for them? What happens if you live, but lose your capacity to earn money and support them?

In short, you've spent years accumulating the wealth that you have. Before you can bequeath it, however, you should protect it. Organize and shelter your assets because, well, the taxman is always waiting in the wings with his hand out, and we never know what events may come our way that can rapidly deplete wealth.

We'll be talking about *protecting all the wealth you've acquired through living trusts*—those legal vehicles designed to protect not just physical assets or cash for yourself and your heirs, but all of your property and your right to control its distribution no matter what happens.

We'll be talking about *protecting all the wealth you've acquired through living trusts*—those legal vehicles designed to protect not just physical assets or cash for yourself and your heirs.

You might believe that if you have a will (aka a Last Will and Testament) to say who gets your beloved stamp collection and your six-year-old car, that your estate planning is complete. We'll show you that you might need more than that.

Living Trusts vs. Wills

Understanding the terminology also means you get clear about the differences among the strategies you need to consider. Most people have a will, but many do not understand the benefits of setting up a trust.

The difference between a living trust and a will (also sometimes called a *last will and testament*) is crucial because choosing the right tool can make all the difference in how smoothly your estate is not only managed but also transferred to your heirs.

Many assume that wills and trusts are interchangeable, but they serve different purposes. Both documents state the 'who gets what' piece of your planning.

Wills as a basic estate planning tool are simple but more limited than trusts. They allow you to name who will inherit your assets after your death; name guardians for your minor and/or special needs children; and you appoint an executor (this is the equivalent of a trustee in a trust) to carry out your wishes.

However, a will does not avoid probate. Your estate must go through the court-supervised probate process if all you have is a will, which can take months (or even years). Your financial business becomes public record. Each state may require a separate probate proceeding if you own property in multiple states.

A will is often enough for simple estates or for situations where the primary concern is appointing a guardian for minor children. When your primary goals are to avoid legal delays around passing on your assets and to protect privacy, a living trust is a far more effective solution.

A living trust allows you to avoid probate (even with assets in two or more states), allowing assets to pass to your beneficiaries quickly and privately. You manage your assets during your lifetime without court intervention, including in case of illness or incapacity (which often results in a 'conservatorship') because you have named a trustee who manages the affairs related to the property in the trust.

Your affairs remain private since trusts do not become public records, except in very rare circumstances. And of course you control how your assets are distributed to your beneficiaries. This means you may set conditions for heirs to receive their bequests. The 'how and when' of distribution is up to you. For example, you may establish that your children receive funds only at a certain age; funds are distributed as annuities over many years.

Rest easy; you don't need to memorize every technical term or definition to talk intelligently with your advisors. You now have most of it! The process of wealth management can be a breeze once you have the basics.

As we go along, we'll also show you *why* you might need the protection of one or more trusts. They are not just for material assets but can also protect *your dependents and other heirs.* Many smart people hesitate to start the protective ball rolling. It's emotional for two main reasons.

1. First, people's thoughts immediately go to their own death, and they shiver. No one likes to think about their own demise!

2. They foresee legal complexities, paperwork, and tough choices. And face it: if you decide to craft your living trust yourself with a web-based application, you still have to make the tough decisions.

One of those decisions, if you are married, is about taking care of the surviving spouse. How do you do that with a trust? You can, and there are a few ways to do that. But really, if you want to make sure that what you have earned is a tool and not just a handout to the taxman, then trusts are for you. They give you the ability to control your wealth in a way that you would not otherwise have. So, this is what this book aims to do: give you control of your money no matter what happens.

Stepping into this world filled with legal jargon, endless paperwork, and decisions we are tempted to put off for another day is nothing like our earning days, when our decisions were more about "What does my take-home pay look like if I max out my 401(k) contributions?"

So ... how about we make it simpler for you? So much to learn! Keep on reading. We wrote this book to educate you. Education is power—and we firmly believe in it, which is why we wrote this book—we hope it will lessen fears and reduce our "What-Ifs". Understanding also leads us to the right action to achieve your own determined goals, and that is what you want.

Throughout these pages, we will share ***How It Works*** stories about people who are creating or updating their living trusts and estate plans. John and Mary are the first for you.

How It Works

John and Mary believed they had done everything right. Married for thirty-five years, they had built a life they were proud of. Their home was paid off, their investments were stable, and they had saved diligently, assuming that when the time came, things would fall into place.

Then John passed away—suddenly, and for Mary, far too suddenly to understand their financial affairs. The belief that everything was "taken care of" proved incomplete.

Instead of being able to grieve in her own time, Mary found herself buried in paperwork, trying to piece together what John had done to organize their finances. Some accounts were jointly held; others were not. The mutual fund account was solely in John's name, forcing her into a maze of legal procedures just to gain access—along with the added challenge of locating passwords and online records.

She faced unfamiliar forms, unexpected requirements, and a growing sense that something essential was missing. What had once been a life built together now felt like a puzzle she was left to solve alone.

This happens more often than we'd like to admit, and we don't want that to be you!

Yes, people are concerned about protecting their families, but we believe there's always time—that these things will sort themselves out, and that 'everybody knows what they need to know'. For those of you who are married, there's an untested certainty that your spouse 'will be able to figure it out' or 'will know what to do from our many conversations'. Those assumptions are too often false.

Some wrongly assume estate planning is:

- Just for the rich and old
- Only for those with more stuff
- Something that can wait and be done next year

Not so! Estate planning to put your affairs in order starts the moment you earn money, and for most of you, that was back in your teens or twenties. Surely you named a beneficiary on your very first bank account. Then you should also have been guided to name a beneficiary on your company-sponsored retirement accounts or your pension plan. The action of naming beneficiaries is a part of 'estate planning', and most people don't realize it.

So, yes—estate planning is for you, too, and not just those anonymous rich folks out there. The best time to put those affairs in order is now.

10 Bonus Planning Tools & Worksheets

Congratulations on taking the first step toward protecting your legacy!

As a thank you for reading *Complete Living Trust Blueprint*, I've created an exclusive collection of bonus materials to speed up your estate planning journey. These downloadable resources turn the knowledge you've gained into actionable results.

Get Instant Access Now

90-Day Roadmap for Completing Your Living Trust

"Only put off until tomorrow what you are willing to die having left undone." — ***Pablo Picasso***

This **90-Day Plan** walks you through the entire process in clear, manageable steps. You don't need a law degree, a large budget, or specialized financial or legal expertise to understand what's involved. The plan also gives you the clarity to evaluate an attorney's guidance if you choose to work with one. Its purpose is not to push you toward a single approach, but to ensure you understand your options well enough to make sound, confident decisions.

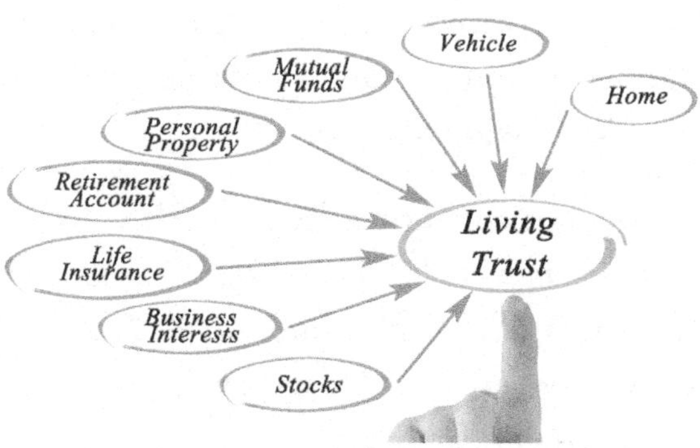

In this book, you will find:

- A step-by-step guide to your part in setting up your living trust.
- An explanation of the terminology you'll hear from professional legal and tax advisors. This will allow you to ask informed questions and understand the answers.
- Some trust strategies to protect your assets, minimize taxes, and maximize your legacy for your heirs.
- A few ideas, tools, and strategies for those who want to Do-It-Yourself as much as possible.
- Stories (***How It Works***) about how people benefited from proactive estate planning (and a few cautionary tales from those who did not).
- Let's face it: you are smart enough to have accumulated some wealth. We don't care how old you are right *now*. *Now* is the right time to be smart about protecting it, protecting your loved ones, and sleeping with peace of mind every night.

When the unexpected happens (and it will, as almost everyone you can name will attest), you want to ensure that your loved ones are cared for, and not left sorting through a mass of paperwork like Mary when she was suddenly widowed.

As you read these pages, we'll be answering the questions we know you have: *Do I really need a living trust, or is a will enough? What happens if I* do nothing *and die tomorrow? How complicated and time-consuming is this going to be? How can I really be sure my spouse, kids, and grandkids are protected?*

Protecting your legacy shouldn't be a burden, and won't be once you start this step-by-step process we present. It will prove one of the smartest, most loving decisions you've ever made.

Your Purpose, Your Education

Week 1: Education; Your Goals & Needs

- Read and review this entire book. (Twelve chapters)
    - Note how you might use this information for your living trust or a larger estate plan.
    - Note your questions for an attorney or further reading on your own.
- Define your primary goals for the living trust and a larger estate plan. (Chapter 2)
    - Does your plan need to protect assets—and which ones?
    - Does your plan need to create more tax efficiency?
    - Does your plan need to protect certain heirs—and why?
- Start writing up your asset inventory. (Chapter 2)
    - Consider all types of assets.
    - Note them as they come to mind.

Week 2: Family Dynamics Assessment

- Start discussions with your spouse/partner about shared goals, current and future needs, and what happens in the estate plan when one predeceases the other. (Chapter 2)

    - What aspects do you disagree about? Why? What is the agreed-upon solution?
    - Commit to working on this plan together so that you both possess the same information and know where to find the documents you create when needed.

- Consider other family relationships and potential challenges of bequeathing to some and not to others, and why. (Chapters 2 & 9)
- Start thinking about who gets what (your heirs/beneficiaries). (Chapter 9)
- Who would you name as guardians for your minor children? (Chapters 1 & 9).
- Who would you name as a Power of Attorney for financial and for healthcare matters (two people) (Chapter 6)?
- Assuming you name yourself as trustee during your lifetime, who would you name as successor trustee after your passing? (Chapter 3)

Professional Engagement and Planning

Week 3: Select and Meet With Professionals

- Decide if you need professional guidance and then identify local estate planning attorneys (those specializing in estate planning and trusts) if so (Chapters 5 & 6).

    - Who can refer you to an attorney they know/have consulted (i.e. someone you can trust)?

- Interview two-three attorneys (Chapter 6).
    - Choose and schedule the initial consultation.
- Bring financial documents and your asset inventory list to your first meeting.
    - Come with your questions about trust structure, fees, and timeline.
    - Discuss state-specific issues (Chapter 5).

Week 4: Trust Design and Strategy

- Determine the best trust structure for your needs.
    - Does the attorney suggest one or more types of living trusts to fulfill your purposes and goals? Discuss the functions, pros, and cons (Chapter 10).
- Discuss tax implications with a financial advisor/accountant (Chapter 10).
    - Arrange a meeting with you and together with tax and legal advisors.
- Strategy is also who your beneficiaries, Power of Attorney agents, and trustees will be.
    - Name beneficiaries and how/when distributions are made (Chapter 9).

- Begin drafting trust instructions on your own (Chapter 7) and with professional guidance (all Chapters).

Document Creation and Asset Organization

Weeks 5-6: Trust Document Creation

- Review and refine trust documents.
- Decide on specific provisions and contingencies.
- Create a pour-over will to complement your trust (Chapter 10).
- Draft powers of attorney for healthcare directives (for medical decision-making) and for financial affairs.

Weeks 7-8: Asset Documentation and Preparation

- Compile all asset documentation (deeds, titles, account statements).
- Update beneficiary designations on financial accounts according to their in-house rules.
- Besides the detailed inventory of your valuable personal property, including digital assets, that you compiled in Weeks 1 and 2.
    - Get new valuations/appraisals for each item.
    - Date and document valuations/appraisals for each of your valuables—jewelry, real estate, art, etc. (Chapter 2)

Implementation and Finalization

Weeks 9-10: Trust Funding

- Start transferring real estate into the trust (Chapter 1).
- Re-title financial accounts in the name of your trust, with the aid of professionals as needed.
- Update vehicle titles and other personal property.
- Ensure digital assets are properly documented for how to access and manage them (Chapter 4).

Week 11: Review and Communication

- Review the entire trust package:
    - Ask for needed explanations; ask any outstanding questions.
    - The attorney should have explained how documents become not just filed but legally recognized in court.
    - Double-check all witness signatures (as required for the trust or document in your state), your signature, and notarization as required for all documents. (Chapters 6 & 9)
    - Double-check that all institutions (and you) have fully transferred to the trust all assets to be protected. (Chapter 6)
- Schedule a meeting with your designated (successor)

trustee(s).

- Optional: Create a letter of intent for beneficiaries (Chapter 9)

Week 12: Finalization and Storage

- Create secure storage systems for your trust documents: paper and/or digital?
- Ensure your spouse and/or successor trustees will have access to the documentation.
- Share essential information with the trustees.
- Schedule periodic trust reviews.
- Make necessary periodic updates to your documents (beneficiary, trustee, asset changes, etc.)

As You Prepare

Creating a living trust often leads to a broader estate plan shaped by your individual goals and circumstances. While estate planning is always personal, the steps in the 90-Day Roadmap cover the essential groundwork that applies to everyone. At a minimum, they will help you ask the right questions of an estate planning professional.

If you are married, stay informed and involved together throughout the process. Agree on the terms of your trust and ensure you both know where documents are stored and how to access them when needed. Choose a storage solution that keeps your trust documents secure, confidential, and accessible to both of you.

Chapter One

Basics of Living Trusts

"If you do not have a Will or plan for your estate, then the government has one for you." — ***Shez Christopher***

When someone passes away without a will, a situation known as dying intestate, the responsibility for distributing their assets falls to the court. The court follows a standard set of rules intended to be fair, but those rules are impersonal by nature and may not reflect individual wishes, family relationships, or timing concerns. For the people left behind, this process can be both costly and stressful. In uncommon cases, when no legal heirs are identified, assets may ultimately revert to the state.

Estate planning, often described as putting one's affairs in order, is really about clarity and intention. It begins with understanding what you own and deciding what should happen to it, both during your lifetime and after. That includes identifying your assets, choosing who should receive them, and determining when and how those transfers take place, while you continue to use and enjoy what you have worked to build. At its best, estate planning is not about paperwork or legal terminology, but about making thoughtful decisions in advance so others do not have to make them for you later.

This book focuses on one of the most practical tools for creating that clarity: the living trust. A living trust allows you to organize your assets, maintain control over them during your lifetime, and provide clear instructions for what happens next. Used thoughtfully, it can simplify the transfer process, reduce delays and expenses, and offer peace of mind for you and for the people you care about. The chapters that follow will walk you through how living trusts work, when they make sense, and how to decide whether one fits your situation.

Estate planning is your way of ensuring that the people you love are cared for without unnecessary stress, legal battles, or financial headaches. This planning not only gives you peace of mind, but it also provides comfort, clarity, and peace of mind for your heirs.

Over the years, you have mapped out your financial and material journey—earning, saving, investing, and gaining material wealth. If you are reading this book, we presume you did that not only to enjoy a comfortable retirement but also to leave those you love (and/or charitable causes you are passionate about) some form of legacy. That's what this book is designed to help you achieve.

A living trust ensures that transferring your wealth, your financial assets, your material property, and other possessions to your beneficiaries happens efficiently, without unnecessary legal or financial delays. A well-designed living trust manages the details with clarity, not only for your loved ones but also stands up (if it should come to that) in a court of law.

Your family can enjoy what you've built, free from stress.

What Is a Living Trust?

As you will see in this book, different types of Trusts exist to help people protect, manage, and pass on their assets, but also to protect the people they love. You won't need all the types of trust that exist, but you'll consider at least one.

There are four categories of trust: **Living trusts** (our topic in this book); **Testamentary trusts** (you create these now but, like a **Last will**, they are only activated upon your death—not our topic here); **Revocable trusts** (ones allowing you to change the terms and contents after you've drafted them); and **Irrevocable trusts** (ones not allowing you to change the terms and contents).

Why This Book Focuses on Living Trusts
Living trusts are the most commonly used trust structure in everyday estate planning because they offer flexibility, control, and practical protection during your lifetime. Most living trusts are **revocable**, meaning you can change the terms, update beneficiaries, or move assets in and out of the trust as your life circumstances change. This combination of control and adaptability makes living trusts especially appealing to individuals and families who want to avoid probate, plan for incapacity, and keep their estate plan current without locking themselves into permanent decisions. Other types of trusts exist, but they are typically designed for more specific or advanced situations and are best addressed separately with professional guidance.

A living trust is a legal document that transfers ownership of your assets to a trust. Then a trustee, named by the creator of the trust, manages the assets on your behalf and for your chosen beneficiaries. You can name yourself or a loved one as "trustee," which is discussed further below, or an institutional professional. In this way, you can protect your assets while retaining an important degree of control over them.

If your living trust benefits heirs who are all family members, this is also called a **family trust**. Here too, you transfer ownership of your assets to the trust. It's just that all beneficiaries you name will be family members.

Yes, you *transfer ownership* of your assets. If you already have a will and beneficiary designations on your financial accounts, setting up a trust might sound like it adds complexity—or isn't even needed. But here's the truth: A living trust isn't about giving up control; *it's about having more of it.*

A living trust is valid and active and protects your assets during your lifetime provided you set it up correctly (explained later in this book). However, a simple last will and testament cannot do that, as it takes effect only upon your death. During your life, a living trust lets you manage your assets exactly how you want. A living trust does this without court delays (usually, there is no need to go to court at all), extra fees, or family misunderstandings about what your wishes were and are.

Think of this trust as a secure box with your name on it where you keep your valuable, hard-earned assets safe. You still have the keys. You can move items in or out, change instructions, or even dissolve the trust (when this is a *revocable* trust, as defined above). Only when the time comes can your family and other heirs access what you've set aside for them.

It's not about complicating things; it's about making life easier—for you and the people you love.

The Three Key Players in a Living Trust

A living trust involves three key roles—and if you're setting one up, you are already the most important one:

- **Grantor:** You are the grantor as it's you who has created the trust, decided how it works, and transferred your assets into it.

- **Trustee:** This is the person who manages the trust. This will also be your role while you are alive (except in cases we will describe later). In your trust documents, you name a 'successor' trustee who takes over upon your passing, and a 'back-up' trustee to step in if/when you cannot make your own decisions anymore. (More on the trustee's role in Chapter 2).

- **Beneficiary:** The individuals or organizations you choose to receive your assets—family, friends, or charitable organizations. When you document the 'who gets what', this is called '*beneficiary designation*'. What the beneficiary receives is called a '*bequest*'. (More on beneficiaries in Chapter 9).

What Transferring Assets Means

Transferring assets to the trust is also called '*funding the trust*'.

You are not transferring your assets per se; you are simply re-titling them (meaning that you are changing ownership from yourself personally to the trust as an independent entity). For real property, you rewrite (usually with the guidance of your attorney or a DIY tool) the deed; for financial accounts, you change account ownership to the trust (the banker or financial institution will assist you). The process is similar for DMV-registered vehicles. For property without ownership papers, your attorney will list and describe such transfers in your trust documents.

Instead of being under your own name, "Jane Doe," your home becomes the property "Jane Doe, Trustee of the Jane Doe Living Trust." In fact, while the trust owns it, you control it.

We must remind you that without a trust (and even if you have a properly drafted will), your estate must go through a court hearing called probate. It's expensive. Your heirs may not understand the process. It is not private. With a trust, however, your affairs don't go to probate; your business remains private; your successor trustee can distribute your assets privately and efficiently, just as you intend.

Transferring your assets into a *revocable* living trust means you still have control. You can change who your beneficiaries will be; you can change trustees; you can adjust the terms of distribution of your assets (that is, decide or change when and how your possessions will go to a beneficiary). You can update your revocable living trust at any time and many times.

- **Revocable Living Trust**: Its terms can be fully changed while you are alive. This means you can update beneficiaries, name different trustees, add/remove assets, or cancel the trust entirely. Changes need proper documenting in an '*amendment*' or '*schedule*'. This trust avoids probate and simplifies estate management in the case of your incapacity or inability to manage your affairs yourself. However, it does not offer asset protection from creditors nor estate tax advantages.

While an *irrevocable* (that is, not changeable once created and funded) trust is more rigid, it provides stronger asset protection and tax advantages. You might choose this form of trust depending on your specific situation; a trained attorney knows the questions to ask to determine which category of living trust you need. Review your DIY trust document with an attorney, especially if your assets or wishes are complex.

- **Irrevocable Trust**: Its terms should be considered permanent and unchangeable (or at least very time-consuming and costly in court proceedings to modify) once established and funded. It provides stronger protection from creditors (and that spouse you are divorcing) and potential estate tax savings. It is best considered for high-value estates or specific planning needs (we will look at some of those later).

Benefits of Establishing a Living Trust

There are four big advantages to you of creating (writing up in the correct language and form) and activating (funding by re-titling) a living trust. In short, they are 1) no probate court, 2) privacy, 3) asset protection, and 4) potential tax advantages.

Let's recap and look closer at this.

1. Avoid Probate

A living trust bypasses probate to validate your wishes and make sure your heirs get what you want them to.

- 'Probate' is a legal process. You go to court. It requires legal counsel. It costs money and time. The purpose of probate is to validate a will and other claims to your assets after your passing. Probate is about distributing assets to the rightful heirs under court supervision. It comes with delays in your heirs getting their legacy.

- Your living trust allows your trustee to transfer your assets to your beneficiaries directly and immediately, with no court approval. Having a living trust simply means that your whole bequest reaches the people you intended—no fuss, no muss.

2. Privacy

We've said it: unlike a will, which becomes public once it enters probate, a living trust remains confidential. This means there is no public record of what you own, no disclosure of who inherits what, and no opportunity for unwanted parties to challenge your estate in court.

In a world of computer access to so much so-called private information, your financial affairs truly remain private with a living trust.

3. Protection in Case of Incapacity

With a living trust protecting your assets, you are also protecting yourself. If you become ill or unable to manage your affairs, who would step in? Your trustee.

Without a trust or trustee, your loved ones might have to go through the courts to establish a 'conservatorship'. Like probate, this requires a court proceeding and can take a long time indeed, as it determines who will manage your affairs and decide in your place.

Your living trust manages the unpredictable: you've eliminated this uncertainty. You've named a trusted individual (the trustee) or institution to manage your assets if you become incapacitated. This ensures that your finances continue to be handled timely and carefully; court intervention is avoided; your loved ones know who and how your business is being managed.

4. Strategic Tax Planning

Why worry about taxes? Do you really want to have a bigger chunk of your wealth going to taxes when you pass away rather than your heirs? Probably not!

Living trusts don't reduce estate taxes, but are part of broader tax strategies.

Always consult a tax expert to learn about ways to protect your wealth from unnecessary taxes. Ask these professionals about how to defer taxes on certain assets until distribution and understand strategic gifting and giving to maximize what your beneficiaries receive.

Discuss your potential tax obligations in the various scenarios your professional advisors present to you. Income generated by trust assets may still be taxable, so understand how this applies to your estate planning choices. Make sure your tax advisor has your estate structured to minimize taxes.

How It Works

A retired teacher, Sarah consulted an attorney to set up a living trust and transferred her home and savings into it. She named herself as the trustee, keeping full control, and appointed her son Mark as the successor trustee.

Her named heirs are her two children and three grandchildren, with instructions that the grands will receive their inheritance at age twenty-five.

The benefit to them all? Sarah's family avoids probate, saving time and legal costs. Her wishes are honored without court involvement or need for her heirs to pay attorneys and hefty legal fees to claim their legacy. Her grandchildren's bequests are protected until they're old enough to manage them.

This is the power of a living trust. Plan now so your family doesn't struggle later.

Chapter Two

Setting Up Your Living Trust

"*By failing to plan, you are preparing to fail.*" — ***Benjamin Franklin***

Imagine waking up to find your financial world in perfect order—each asset accounted for and each detail carefully planned. There's no scrambling to locate documents, no worrying about legal red tape, and, most importantly, no uncertainty about what will happen to your estate when you're no longer here.

Now, picture your loved ones waking up one day after you're gone. They are (one may assume!) grieving your passing. But they are not tearing their hair out wondering what the next practical step is around closing out your financial and worldly affairs, claiming their bequests, and taking care of each other.

You've eliminated their need for probate, court delays, and legal fees. They have your estate and trust documents. They have immediate access to their bequests—exactly as you intended.

Having a living trust in place achieved all that. To get to that reality, your first step is to list your assets and define your goals.

What Do You Own?

You cannot bequeath it to an heir until you are clear about what you possess. It's time to take an inventory of everything you own—not just the large items, but the small (and sometimes overlooked) ones as well.

As you list all the items with the help of the memory-jogging suggestions below, also ask: "What possessions of mine will my family and loved ones want that I'm not thinking about right now as a valuable asset? What have I told people about 'having my stuff'?"

How It Works

> Jack was a career Army officer who passed away at 92. Over the years, he'd told three different male members of his family that they could have his medals as keepsakes. He never documented those bequests. That led the three men into a heated moment of "He said-But he told me-Not you but me!" and it took another family member to sort things out to mutual satisfaction.

Tangible Assets (What You Can See and Touch)

- **Your home:** whether it's a house, condo, or apartment, this is one of the biggest assets in most people's estates.

- **Other real estate/property:** a cabin in the mountains? A family beach house? Perhaps an empty plot you've been holding onto? List them.

- **Personal valuables:** Think beyond real estate: jewelry, art, RVs, boats, classic cars, and collectibles (baseball cards, vintage records, coins, etc.). These items may hold both sentimental and financial value. For example, if you have an heirloom wedding ring, do you want it passed down through generations, or would you prefer it to be sold with the money divided among your children? These are the kinds of decisions that a trust allows you to specify.

Intangible Assets (What You Own on Paper or Digitally)

- **Bank accounts:** checking, savings, money market accounts; pension accounts when you have opted for survivorship payments.

- **Investments:** stocks, bonds, mutual funds, retirement accounts (e.g. IRA, 401k).

- **Business ownership:** If you own a company, even partially, it's critical to determine what happens to it.

- **Insurance policies:** life insurance payouts (i.e., beneficiary designations) should align with your estate plan.

- **Digital assets:** cryptocurrency ownership, online or digitally managed businesses (websites, Amazon stores, affiliate marketing businesses, etc.). Consider your social media accounts (yes, people leave instructions on what to do with their Facebook or Instagram accounts after they're gone!).

This last item might present the most challenges unless your activity is already organized as a corporation (LLC or other). If you've built a successfully monetized Etsy shop, YouTube channel, or Amazon store, it might continue generating income long after you're gone. Who should manage it? Where should the earnings go? A trust lets you plan for these details.

Your Goals and Wishes

Now that you have a clear picture of what you own, it's time to question what you want to happen to these assets. This is the 'who gets what', but it's also about how and when your heirs will receive your bequests.

- Do you want to protect your wealth for future generations? Perhaps your children are very well off, but you want to ensure that your grandchildren receive financial support at different stages of life (education, buying a home, etc.). You can craft the trust to achieve this.

- Do you own property in two states or more? Each state may require separate probate proceedings without a trust, adding unnecessary costs and delays. A trust eliminates this hassle. Make sure your attorney adds the out-of-state property correctly (each state can have different rules).

- Do you have a business as a sole owner? Are you a partner in one? You'll want to protect it. If you run a family business, a trust ensures it doesn't fall into the wrong hands or get sold off unexpectedly.

- If you are a partner, discuss a written '*partnership agreement*' between you and your partner (s). That might be where your partner is granted 'first option' to purchase your share of the business from your heirs in the case of your incapacity or passing. Don't underestimate its value!

Other Estate Planning Tools You May Encounter

As you think through who should receive your assets, you may come across simpler estate-planning tools such as **transfer-on-death (TOD) or payable-on-death (POD) designations**, as well as **joint ownership arrangements**, like joint tenancy with right of survivorship. These options can allow certain assets—such as bank accounts, investment accounts, or a primary residence—to pass directly to a named individual without going through probate.

While these tools can be helpful in limited situations, they are **incomplete solutions** for most comprehensive estate plans. They typically apply only to specific assets, offer little control over *how* or *when* beneficiaries receive funds, and do not address incapacity, blended families, minor beneficiaries, or multi-state property. In addition, joint ownership can create unintended consequences, including loss of control, exposure to a co-owner's creditors, or conflicts among heirs.

A living trust brings these individual pieces together into a coordinated plan. Rather than relying on separate instructions scattered across accounts and deeds, a trust allows you to clearly define your wishes, provide protections across generations, and ensure your estate is managed consistently—during your lifetime and beyond.

How It Works

> Jeff was in such a case. He had two children, but only one was actively involved in the family business. Because it was family, Jeff rejected the idea of a partnership agreement. Then, his son started slacking on the job! He discussed this with his estate attorney and came up with a solution. We won't tell you what it is, except to say that his son woke up and started carrying his weight in the business again!

Whatever your situation, ask yourself whether you should split any property equally among several heirs. If you proceed in that manner, do you want to ensure that the other children receive an equivalent share of your other assets or through some other type of bequest? There are no rules, really. But there are family dynamics.

Family Dynamics

No one ever said it would be easy to decide the 'who gets what' part of this estate planning. Things can get emotional because families and family relationships are complex, and money often makes things even more complicated. A well-thought-out trust helps avoid conflicts before they arise. Ask yourself:

- Are there potential disputes, bad blood among heirs?

- If one child cares for you in your later years, while others are wholly or absent, should they inherit equally? Remember that you are the decision-maker of the 'who gets what and how', and the living trust makes it clear to all involved.

- Do you need to set conditions for an inheritance? If you're worried about an heir squandering their inheritance, a trust allows you to release funds gradually or as an annuity (which the trust owns). You should also ask your attorney about a '***spendthrift trust***' (see Chapter 10 for details on this and other types of special-purpose living trusts).

- Are there blended-family considerations? If you have children, stepchildren, an ex-spouse, a current spouse—a trust ensures they all understand without dispute what you have bequeathed to them.

How It Works

> John remarried in his sixties and wants to make sure his new wife is taken care of if he passes away first. However, he also wants to ensure that his children from his first marriage inherit a significant portion of his estate. A living trust allows him to provide for both parties with no uncertainty.

Key Elements of a Trust Document

Creating a living trust isn't just about signing a boilerplate document that looks like everyone else's living trust. Your trust is customized. It's your voice when you are no longer here to decide, so every detail matters.

Think of it as writing the ultimate instruction manual for your estate. Who gets what? When? How? Under what conditions? Who is to make sure it happens as written?

These are the critical questions your trust must answer—clearly and without room for misunderstanding. Here is how your attorney will draft a trust agreement that truly protects your legacy.

Note that if you choose to Do-It-Yourself with a trust-creator software (more on those in Chapter 7), the key elements of your trust document will be the same.

Step 1: The Main Players

As previously discussed, even if you are both grantor and trustee, the attorney will need to know who your beneficiaries and chosen successor trustee are to be. You'll need to know the assets to protect and the title to the trust.

How It Works

> Emma, a widow with two adult children, sets up a living trust as a grantor. She names herself as the initial trustee and her eldest son, Michael, as the successor trustee. Her trust ensures that her younger son, Jake, receives his inheritance in structured payments instead of a lump sum. Jake has an unresolved gambling addiction; Emma worries about his financial discipline. She set it up as an annuity owned by the trust, with monthly payments to Jake's bank account that are enough to pay a rent or mortgage and feed him. This setup protects both her assets and her son's future.

Step 2: Your Assets

You've probably been assembling the list of your assets since you started reading this book. It's always good to start early on this exercise because your trust can only protect and later bequeath the assets you place into it. A vague or incomplete memory can lead to a vague and incomplete trust document, which ends up not protecting the assets or the heirs in the manner intended by you.

How It Works

> Mark has a large investment portfolio (only stocks) and a rental property (a four-plex apartment building), and some cash savings. He keeps it fairly simple as these things go. He specifies in his trust that:
>
> - His rental income will go in entirety to his wife for the rest of her life. The four-plex is held in the trust and goes to his children in equal shares after his spouse's death.
> - His stock investments will be liquidated 'at market value' upon his death, the trading account closed, and the funds divided equally between his two children.
> - The cash in his other financial accounts will go to his spouse.
>
> Mark ensures that his assets are distributed exactly as he envisioned by being specific and intentional.

Step 3: Define How Assets Will Be Distributed

'Who inherits what' is one decision, but 'how and when' they inherit is just as important. In reading, Emma created a 'how and when' for her gambling son. There are other possibilities:

- Outright Distribution**:** This is the simplest method, and exactly what Mark has done. Beneficiaries receive their inheritances promptly. It is best suited to financially responsible adults.
- **Staggered Distributions:** Instead of a lump sum, ben-

eficiaries receive payments over time (e.g., 30% at age 25, another 30% at age 30, and the rest at age 35).

- **Conditional Distributions:** Funds are released only when certain conditions are met (e.g., college graduation with a Bachelor's degree from an accredited school; sobriety milestones; a five-year history of full-time employment).

How It Works

> Rachel wants to leave a trust fund to her daughter Olivia. She worries, though, about Olivia's history of reckless spending. Instead of an outright gift, she sets conditions in the trust. First, Olivia will receive money from the trust only for college tuition and living expenses while studying. Rachel states that the tuition will be paid by the trust directly to the school. Second, Olivia will gain full control of the trust at age 35—but only if Rachel shows to the trustee that she has 1) held down a full-time job consistently and 2) proves her financial management skills are solid. An additional condition is that if Olivia ever struggles with addiction, funds can be paused or redirected to a rehabilitation program. This is a situation where I would definitely get legal advice. You may find that state or federal laws could create issues with this type of management, and decline certain state or federal benefits if a trust has such language.

A well-structured trust ensures that assets support beneficiaries—not enable poor decisions. This is a consideration for many parents. I have chosen not to manage from the grave; I give to both my children equally. This is a contentious issue with my spouse; starting early allows for more options.

Step 4: The Unexpected

None of us has a crystal ball to read into the future or that of anyone else. Your revocable living trust has the flexibility to adapt to unforeseen events.

- What happens if your successor trustee is unwilling or unable to serve? You have already named a backup trustee.
- What if a beneficiary predeceases you? You have already stated that the bequest is to be re-aggregated and re-divided among the new number of beneficiaries or given to a contingent beneficiary.
- What if one of your heirs becomes disabled and requires specialized financial care? You set up an emergency trust that becomes effective in that case, but otherwise lies dormant.

How It Works

> James initially names his best friend, David, as his successor trustee. However, David and James had an irreparable falling out four or five years after funding his trust. His trust already had a secondary or backup trustee listed, his niece Serina, who has just confirmed that she is willing and able to step in. James's trust is revocable, so he removes David, names Serina as the new primary successor trustee, and adds a new backup trustee he has identified and spoken with.

Step 5: Ensure Your Trust Is Legally Rock-Solid

Even the most carefully written trust won't hold up if it is not legally compliant. That's what estate attorneys do all day. Trust issues, such as poor drafting or outdated provisions, result in litigation. Or rather, your heirs go to court.

How It Works

> Linda drafted and funded a living trust ten years ago, naming her then-husband as her primary beneficiary. After their divorce, she simply forgot to update her living trust beneficiary. When she passed away, the trust still named her ex-husband as the principal heir—and it was legally binding. This resulted in a bitter family dispute.

Chapter Three

Choosing A Trustee and Funding Your Trust

"*Give your kids enough so they can do anything, but not so much that they'll do* nothing." — ***Warren Buffett***

Choosing the right trustee isn't just about checking off a box in your estate plan—it's about selecting the person (or entity) who will uphold your wishes, protect your assets, and act in the best interest of your loved ones long after you're gone. Consider your trustee to be the leader steering your financial matters, making wise decisions, and ensuring the smooth distribution of your assets to your beneficiaries. Pick the wrong captain; your estate plan could face mismanagement, disputes, and even legal battles.

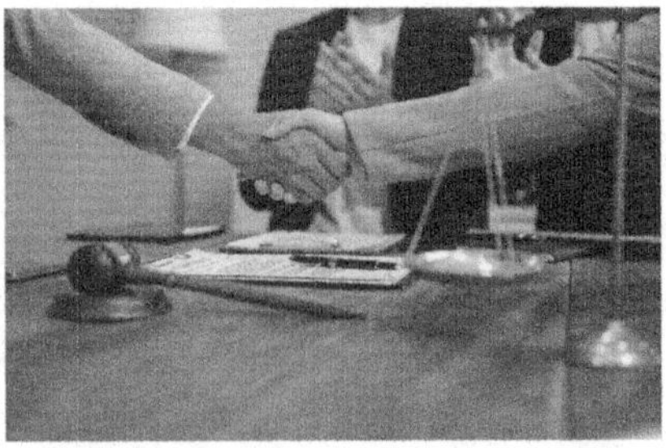

What Does a Trustee Do?

A trustee isn't just a title on a document—it's a real person who has real, day-to-day responsibilities that impact your beneficiaries' financial future. These responsibilities include:

- **Managing assets:** investing wisely, protecting property, and ensuring that assets grow rather than dwindle unnecessarily.
- **Following the trust's instructions:** distributing money or property exactly as outlined, whether immediately, in installments, or under specific conditions.
- **Keeping records and filing taxes:** documenting financial transactions and handling tax filings to remain compliant.
- **Acting as a mediator (as needed):** If there are disputes between beneficiaries, the trustee may need to step in as a neutral decision-maker.

How It Works

> Donald named his younger brother, Brian, as his successor trustee for his family trust. Brian is great with money but struggles with family dynamics. When Donald passed, Brian's role wasn't just to manage finances; it was also to ensure that Donald's children (and other family members) didn't argue over Donald's assets. Brian found himself caught in the middle of heated family tensions without clear guidance. The lesson here is that the best trustee isn't just good with numbers; they also need to handle family matters with fairness and diplomacy.

Who Makes the Best Trustee?

A trustee doesn't have to be a financial genius, but they must be honest, responsible, ethical, and organized. Look for trustworthiness. You want someone who will carry out your wishes exactly as you intended, not based on their own opinions or personal interests. Look for financial competence. You want someone who possesses a basic understanding of investments, taxes, and legal compliance. They don't need to be Wall Street experts, but they should be capable of making sound financial decisions. Look for neutrality. If you're appointing a family member, choose someone who can remain fair and unbiased (not to mention cool and calm) if conflicts arise. Last, look for willingness and availability. The best trustee in the world is useless if they don't have the time or willingness to handle the responsibility.

How It Works

> Mia, a widowed mother of three, initially considers her oldest daughter, Lisa, as her trustee. Although Lisa is responsible, she also has a demanding job and three children of her own. Instead, Mia chooses her financially savvy younger brother, Tom, knowing he also has more time to handle trust duties and is viewed as neutral among the children.
>
> Mia got it: The obvious choice isn't always the best one or the one with the highest chance of success. It is important to consider time commitment and family dynamics.

Should You Choose a Professional Trustee?

If no one in your family is a good fit—and if you don't want to be your own trustee, or if your estate is large and complex—you might consider hiring a professional trustee (such as a bank, trust company, or lawyer).

There are some advantages to hiring a professional trustee: you get experience and expertise; they understand taxes, legal compliance, and investments. You get impartiality; they won't be swayed by family conflicts or personal biases. You get long-term stability because, unlike an individual, a trust company won't age, move away, or pass away.

There are some drawbacks to hiring a professional trustee: you pay fees; professionals charge for their services, sometimes as a percentage of the trust's assets. The relationship is less personal as a bank or law firm won't know your family as intimately as a relative might (and that might be just what you need!), but get the technical aspects perfectly right.

How It Works

> Raul has a blended family—two adult children from his first marriage and two from his second. He fears that appointing one child as the trustee will lead to resentment from the others. Instead, he names a professional trustee to ensure fairness. He knew that family tensions could be high and that a neutral third party would be the best choice.

Setting Clear Expectations With Your Trustee

Even the best trustee needs guidance. You can avoid misunderstandings and conflicts by outlining clear expectations in your trust. The right trustee is the heart of your trust and can ensure that your assets are handled wisely, prevent family conflicts, and honor your legacy exactly as you envisioned. But choosing the wrong trustee can undo all your careful planning. So, take your time and weigh your options.

Ask yourself: *Who will manage my estate with the same (or better) care I would?* The answer to that question is the right trustee for you. You and the trustee should answer and agree on the following and write up the responses as instructions in the trust document:

- How often should the trustee update beneficiaries? Monthly? Annually?
- What financial reports should they provide? Bank statements? Investment performance reports?
- Who has a say in major decisions? Should beneficiaries have input on significant financial moves?

How It Works

> Rebecca leaves an investment property in her trust, and her successor trustee isn't sure whether to sell it or rent it out. If Rebecca had left instructions (she did not) such as "Sell only if the property value drops below X amount", the trustee wouldn't have to guess. Still, she chose her trustee well, and he made the right decision.

Your trust should be a roadmap, not a puzzle. Clearly outline your wishes; include them all in the trust document.

Fund the Trust

Funding your trust is the critical step that transforms your estate plan into a functional reality, ensuring that your assets are properly managed during your lifetime and passed on smoothly when the time comes.

Step 1: What Goes Into the Trust?

Every asset must be listed in the trust document or it won't be protected. That's first. Your trust can only manage the assets you place into it, so the first step is deciding what should be transferred. You don't need to re-title all your assets to the trust, but you can. Discuss this with your partner/spouse, then the two of you should discuss it with the attorney.

For the best advice, look to your biggest assets first. For many, that means real estate and cash accounts.

Real Estate

For many, their home is their most valuable possession. To ensure it bypasses probate, you need to re-title the deed in the trust's name. For most people, high-value assets mean you'll protect *all your real estate* as a priority, which could include not just your primary residence, but vacation homes, rental properties, or land.

Re-titling the property into the trust's ownership is vital, but there is more:

1. Update the deed to list the trust as the owner
2. Consult a real estate attorney (some states require additional legal steps) and complete the additional steps the attorney lists
3. File the new deed with the county recorder's office

How It Works

> Gina owns a family home in the suburbs and a beautiful cabin in the mountains. Transferring these properties to her trust ensures that Gina's children inherit them immediately without court delays, while also avoiding thousands of dollars in probate fees. To make sure that happens, Gina funds the trust with the newly titled property deeds.

- Your cash/financial accounts are probably the next most valuable asset you have to protect. For some diligent savers, their cash assets surpass the value of their real estate. Whatever the case, protect them. Not all accounts need to be re-titled into the trust, but you need to align them with your estate plan. Fund your trust with checking and savings accounts, investment accounts (stocks, bonds, mutual funds), retirement accounts (IRA, 401(k), etc.), and life insurance policies.

- If some accounts (e.g., checking) are meant for everyday use, you have options. You can either re-title them to the trust (and continue to use them) or name the trust as the payable-on-death (POD) beneficiary. Request the forms for such ownership changes from your financial institution. These should not be re-titled into the trust. However, you name the trust as your beneficiary. The trust can be the primary or secondary beneficiary, ensuring that proceeds are distributed as planned.

How It Works

> Julie has a brokerage account with substantial investments. Instead of leaving it outside the trust—where it would go through probate—she transfers ownership to her trust, allowing her successor trustee to manage and distribute it (per her instructions) without delay upon her passing.

Step 2:

The Paperwork

Transferring assets into your trust isn't automatic; as mentioned above, you need to update legal documents to reflect the change in ownership. Let's review what you've done (and review your actions with your attorney to make sure everything is in order).

- Re-title assets: Real estate, bank accounts, and investments must be legally transferred to the trust's name.

- Update beneficiary designations: Some assets (like retirement accounts) don't go into the trust, but naming the trust as a beneficiary ensures they are distributed correctly.
- Keep detailed records: Maintaining copies of updated documents helps avoid confusion later.

Planning Note: Some assets can pass using transfer-on-death (TOD/POD) designations or joint ownership, which may avoid probate for those specific accounts. However, these tools are limited, offer little control over timing or conditions, and do not address incapacity or more complex family or asset situations. For individuals with multiple assets or growing wealth, a **revocable living trust** provides a more complete and flexible solution.

How It Works

Sean creates a trust but forgets to update his life insurance beneficiary. When he passed, the policy still named his ex-wife—not his children, as he intended.

The beneficiaries named in writing are legally binding; the courts will enforce the documented wishes, not verbal intentions. That is why initial and later periodic reviews and updates of your documents will ensure that you don't make this mistake.

Step 3: Understand Tax Implications

Most transfers into a *revocable* living trust won't trigger taxes; however, *irrevocable* trusts and *substantial asset transfers* may carry tax consequences.

Our tax structure and laws are complex. Therefore, it's important, even if you do DIY planning, that you consult both a tax professional and your estate attorney (preferably in the same room together at least initially, then once a year for reviews). If you're unsure about the tax implications, consult your tax expert *before* making transfers. A little planning can prevent costly mistakes. Thus, even if you want to handle the core aspect of your estate plan on your own, it is a good idea to spend a little time consulting with professionals in the field to be sure you understand the consequences of your choice *in advance.*

As a rule of thumb:

- Revocable trusts: There is no immediate tax impact, but the trust's assets remain a part of your estate.
- Irrevocable trusts: These can assist with estate taxes but require giving up control over the assets.

Step 4: Keep the Trust Updated

Funding your trust isn't a one-and-done task (and yes, you've read this more than once; it's that important!). It requires ongoing maintenance.

- **Review your trust regularly:** Life changes (such as marriage, divorce, or new grandchildren) may require updates.
- **Add new assets:** Newly purchased properties, accounts, or investments should be transferred to the trust immediately. Likewise, if you've sold an asset, remove it.
- **Update valuations:** Periodically have real estate and other high-value property (jewelry, RVs, boats, fur coats, collections and antiques, etc.) appraised and add the appraisal

documents with the new values to your trust documents.

- Adjust beneficiary designations: ensure they still reflect your current wishes and current reality.

How It Works

> Terrence sets up a trust but later buys a vacation home and never transfers it into the trust. When he passes away, his children must go through probate for that one asset, defeating the purpose of the trust. A simple update—an amendment to the trust and re-titling of the property—could have prevented this.

Establishing a living trust is an important step, but ensuring it is properly funded is essential. By transferring assets properly, updating the trust documents to reflect funding, and keeping everything current, you avoid probate headaches for your family, ensure assets are distributed exactly as planned, and maintain privacy and control over your estate. A well-funded trust is one of the most powerful financial tools you can create. Make a point to do regular reviews.

Chapter Four

Avoid the Tax Traps in Estate Planning

"Always plan ahead. It wasn't raining when Noah built the ark." — ***Richard Cushing***

You probably don't even think about taxes in connection with the legacy you're leaving behind. However, if you don't plan carefully, a large portion of your legacy could end up going to taxes instead of benefiting your heirs. I will warn you in advance; the tax stuff is thick. Wade through it the best you can. It is likely you already have a tax accountant; if not, it is a good idea, and they can help with this part.

Estate taxes have been known to eat away at a fortune. To avoid having your hard-earned money ending up paying for tax, you need to do some strategic estate planning. Taxes may seem unavoidable in life (and death), but with proper planning, you can minimize their impact on your hard-earned wealth. The planning we'll be discussing now helps you avoid:

- **Unexpected tax bills:** Your heirs might not have the cash to pay taxes on an inherited property or business, forcing them to sell assets to cover the bill.

- **Delayed access to wealth:** If your estate is taxable, it could take months or years to distribute everything, leaving your loved ones financially stranded.

- Lopsided inheritances: Some beneficiaries might owe more taxes than others, depending on their relationship to you and where they live. (Imagine explaining to your children why one owes more than the other!)

Estate & Inheritance Taxes

Most people don't know that estate taxes and inheritance taxes are two distinct types of taxes.

Estate Tax

- We also call this the 'death tax' (not the most comforting term). It is levied on your estate before your heirs receive anything. Whatever your heirs may receive is net (free) of tax.

- The tax bill is based on the total value of everything you own at the time of your passing—your home, investments, business, and even that classic car you were convinced would appreciate (but which your kids see as an outdated hunk of junk).

Inheritance Tax

- Instead of being taken from the estate before distribution, inheritance taxes are paid by the individuals receiving the assets. It is the heir who pays this tax.

- In some states, the amount taxed depends on how closely the beneficiary is related to the deceased. Immediate family members might pay little to nothing, while distant relatives (or that friend you always joked about leaving everything to) might incur a larger tax bill.

- Federal Estate Tax: The IRS only intervenes if your estate surpasses $13.99 million (as of 2025). You are safe from *federal* estate taxes if your net worth is below that threshold.

- State Estate and Inheritance Taxes: here is where things get tricky. Some states have their own estate or inheritance taxes, and their exemption thresholds are often much lower than the federal limit.

- In a nutshell: Suppose you pass down a $5 million estate to your children. If *estate* taxes apply, they receive their share after taxes are paid by the estate. However, if *inheritance* taxes apply, they inherit the full amount initially and then pay taxes on their end. Either way, Uncle Sam has his hand out and takes a cut.

How It Works

Tom's estate is worth $5 million. He does not have to worry about federal estate taxes, but he lives in a state where the exemption limit is $3 million. This means that $2 million of his estate (the amount over the $3m limit) is taxable at the *state* level—something he would have overlooked entirely, never have even known about, without proper planning.

Steps You Can Take

While estate taxes may seem unavoidable, there are legal, strategic ways to minimize them—or eliminate them altogether. We'll be looking at strategies, including other types of living trusts you can create.

- First (and we've said this) make sure your chosen advisors know about all your assets and, second, get appraisals of all valuables.

- If your estate exceeds the state and/or the federal estate tax exemption ($13.99 million in 2025), be open to the options the tax and trust experts present for both reducing the tax burden and protecting your assets.

- Estate attorneys and tax professionals know how trusts or charitable contributions (discussed in Chapter 10) can help lower your estate's taxable value while protecting your access to your property during your lifetime and for your heirs when you pass away.

How It Works

> Joanne has a $12 million estate and hates that her children will face a hefty tax bill if she doesn't plan. After chatting about strategy with a professional, she begins gifting children, her kids' spouses, and her grandchildren $19,000 each every year (the 2025 IRS limit). She also sets up an irrevocable trust for their future inheritances and donates to charities, both strategies that reduce her taxable estate. Joanne has shaved off millions in potential tax liabilities while ensuring that her heirs receive all she intends.

- As you see, Joanne's yearly gifting is outside a trust. *'Gifting'* is a strategy that happens during your lifetime, and it is one way to reduce your taxable estate while sharing your wealth with beneficiaries during your lifetime. The IRS gifting limit changes annually, so you need to double-check it every year. Note that any gift exceeding that amount or value per person per year is taxable. Spreading out large inheritances over time can effectively reduce your taxable estate (and more on this in later chapters).

Living Trusts and Taxes: Protection and Efficiency

A properly drafted and structured living trust offers a variety of tax advantages that can be crucial in managing an estate tax-efficiently. It is designed for managing, deferring, and even reducing tax obligations that could otherwise reduce your legacy.

- Living trusts, such as ***charitable remainder trusts (CRTs) and grantor-retained annuity trusts (GRATs),*** can remove assets from your taxable estate (we will speak about them in Chapter 10). It will be the trust that owns the assets while ensuring they are distributed exactly as you wish.

Just a word about insurance policies, as people have misconceptions around taxation of the death benefit. There is a living trust to protect that inheritance. A well-structured ***irrevocable life insurance trust (ILIT)*** will own your policy and bypass estate taxes entirely, thus ensuring your loved ones receive the full benefit. However, you need to create the ILIT because if *you* own the policy, the death benefit could still be subject to taxes. Simply fund an ILIT with the policy. The trust as owner removes the policy from your taxable estate, ensuring that beneficiaries receive the full amount tax-free.

One of the biggest advantages of this type of living trust is the ability to *defer* certain tax obligations. Instead of having your heirs face an immediate, lump-sum tax bill due on a large bequest, your trust can be structured to distribute assets gradually, reducing their overall taxable impact.

How It Works

Harold has a $10 million investment portfolio. If everything were passed on all at once, his heirs might be pushed into higher tax brackets, leading to more money lost to taxes. Harold's advisors guide him in drafting trust language that distributes income to each beneficiary over several years, keeping them in lower tax brackets and reducing the total tax paid. When his heirs understood the strategy, they bought into it immediately: Over time; they got more and Uncle Sam got less.

Income Taxes and Trusts: Why Tax Brackets Matter

Many people assume that once assets are placed in a trust, they are automatically taxed less. That is not always the case; it depends on how the trust is structured. Remember that with *revocable* trusts, you keep control, and the IRS still treats the income generated by the trust as your income. This means you are taxed at your normal rate.

It's different with *irrevocable* trusts. Since you no longer 'own' the assets, the trust pays its taxes. However, here is the catch: Trust tax brackets are compressed, meaning they reach the highest tax rate much faster than an individual does.

How It Works

Emiliano leaves in a trust a rental property that generates $50,000 in annual income. If taxed under the trust's bracket, it could face the highest tax rate (37%) after just $15,200 of income. If that income were distributed to his children instead of remaining in the trust, they might pay a much lower rate based on the children's respective tax brackets. His advisors showed him how to keep income inside the trust and when to distribute, and it made all the difference in tax savings to his heirs.

Ralph has a $5 million life insurance policy but realizes that his heirs could owe taxes on the payout if he doesn't plan now. By placing it in an irrevocable life insurance trust (the ILIT), he ensures that the full amount goes directly to his children, untouched by taxes. This trust structure has turned life insurance into a tax-free inheritance instead of a taxable headache.

Capital Gains Tax Loophole

One of the most powerful tax advantages of a living trust is the '***step-up in basis***' rule, which significantly reduces capital gains tax for your heirs.

- **Without a Trust:** If you bought a home for $200,000 decades ago that is now appraised at $700,000, selling the house would produce a $500,000 taxable profit if the heirs sold it. Heirs would owe capital gains tax on the $500,000.

- **With a Trust (and a Step-Up in Basis):** Instead of inheriting the home at your original purchase price and counting the profit as taxable, this does something more tax-efficient for the heir. Before the heir receives the bequest, the home's value is 'stepped-up' to its market value at your passing ($700,000). This eliminates capital gains taxes on past appreciation because that appreciation has been erased.

Instead of gifting these assets during your lifetime (which would keep the original cost basis), you pass them through a trust. When your heirs inherit them, they receive the step-up in basis, meaning they could sell these assets immediately with little to no capital gains tax. If you plan to pass down highly appreciated assets, a living trust can dramatically reduce capital gains tax liability.

How It Works

> Barbara is a retired entrepreneur with a $5 million estate. Among other arrangements in her trust, she wants to ensure her grandchildren's education is covered. Instead of lump sums to each one for this purpose, she gifts each grandchild $19,000 per year. However, instead of going into a normal bank savings account, she sends it into a tax-advantaged (IRS-approved) college savings plan. Over a decade, she has transferred six figures in tax-free education funds to each of them, while lowering her taxable estate. Barbara began this gifting not knowing if she'd see her grandkids start and finish college—but it looks like she is going to be able to do just that!

Trusts are important if you own property. How it's titled can significantly affect what happens after you pass. If you are married, discuss two options with your attorney:

- ***Joint Tenancy with Rights of Survivorship*****:** Property passes directly to the surviving owner, avoiding probate and potentially reducing estate taxes.

- ***Tenancy by the Entirety*** **(for married couples):** This offers even stronger protection against creditors and tax liabilities.

How It Works

Jack and Libbie own their home together as joint tenants. Assuming Jack passes first, when Jack passes away, the property automatically transfers to Libbie's ownership without going through probate. Titling the home in this way saves her time, stress, and legal fees.

Taxes and Keeping Wealth in the Family for Decades

We previously discussed gifting within the annual limit for college funding, and a **Generation-Skipping Transfer (GST) Trust** may also be an option. This type of trust is designed to preserve wealth across multiple generations by directing assets to grandchildren or great-grandchildren rather than passing through children who may already be in higher tax brackets. By skipping a generational transfer, a GST trust can reduce cumulative estate taxes and allow more wealth to remain within the family.

How It Works

Mattie is a grandmother with a $20 million estate. She set up a GST trust to pass wealth directly to her grandchildren. By bypassing her children's taxable estates, she saves the family millions of dollars in potential taxes over multiple generations. Mattie's smart planning today is helping build financial security for future generations of her line.

Chapter Five

Asset Protection and Management

"We make a living by what we get, but we make a life by what we give." — ***Winston Churchill***

We have explored how organizing your assets can protect what you have built and reduce unnecessary taxes, helping your estate pass smoothly to those you love. In this chapter, we focus on the key steps you will take with your spouse or partner and your attorney to strengthen that plan. Clear language and proper documentation are essential, as small gaps can create delays or disputes later. Because estate planning rules vary by state, this chapter emphasizes the importance of getting the details right where you live.

Step 1: Asset Titling and Registration

We've said it: The attorney cannot fund your trust. That's your job. Re-titling each asset is a huge part of the process.

Don't gloss over *how* your assets are titled. If an asset isn't properly registered under your trust, it could get tangled in probate. Just imagine a bureaucratic maze that slows down the transfer process, racks up legal fees, and adds unnecessary stress for your heirs. That's probate court!

If your house (any real estate you own) is still in your name instead of re-titled- to your trust, it won't seamlessly pass to your beneficiaries. Re-title the deed to ensure that it transfers quickly and privately, without court involvement. This is usually done through your county recorder's office or with the help of an estate attorney.

Stocks, bonds, and brokerage accounts should be re-titled in the trust's name to keep them protected. Financial institutions typically require specific forms to update ownership, so make sure you complete the right forms. Then, verify with an agent of the institution that they have recorded the change. This is not the same as designating a beneficiary for each of your accounts—you do that as well.

Step 2: Insure, Insure, Insure—Because Life Is Unpredictable

Just because the trust now owns the assets doesn't mean you stop insuring them! Insurance is your primary safeguard against unforeseen events, whether real estate, art, or an antique collection.

- <u>Homeowners' Insurance</u>: Check with the insurance agent to make sure that the property is covered after its re-titling and transfer into the trust. Review your policy annually, especially if you've made renovations or increased the property's value.

- Valuable Assets Coverage: Standard policies often do not fully cover items such as art, jewelry, or collectibles. If you own high-value items, consider separate riders or specialized policies to ensure complete protection. Check with the insurance carrier to make sure that the property is covered after its re-titling and transfer into the trust.
- Umbrella Liability Insurance: If you have significant assets, this type of insurance adds another layer of security against claims. Discuss the need with both your attorney and your insurance agent.

How It Works

> Geoffrey inherited his grandfather's rare coin collection, which was appraised at several hundred thousand dollars. A break-in left him with a heartbreaking realization: Geoffrey's homeowners' policy didn't cover collectibles beyond a certain value. A simple policy upgrade could have saved him from financial loss.

Don't assume that standard homeowners' insurance covers everything. Review and update your policies regularly with your agent to protect what matters.

Step 3: Diversify Investments

Markets rise and fall, and economic shifts are inevitable, as we've seen more than once in this young millennium. A well-diversified investment portfolio can keep its value growing—no matter what the economy throws your way. It would be wise to consult your financial advisor to diversify your holdings. The advisor is likely to suggest that you:

- Spread risk across asset classes: Real estate, stocks, bonds, and even alternative investments (such as gold or private equity) offer different levels of risk and return.
- Adjust as you age: A younger investor might lean heavily on growth stocks, while someone nearing retirement should prioritize more conservative (slower-growing) instruments.
- Review and rebalance: Like a well-maintained home, your investment strategy requires regular tune-ups to stay aligned with market trends and financial goals.

How It Works

Virginia knew that even though the living trust now owned her portfolio, it would not magically keep up with moves in the market. She had some skill in stock market trading. She regularly reviewed and changed her holdings for the best performance. As she got older, and didn't need to make huge gains anymore, she moved into more 'conservative' stocks that still earned consistently.

Step 4: Know What It's Worth—Keeping Asset Valuations Current

We have mentioned getting periodic appraisals of your high-ticket assets. Consult a jewelry appraiser, a real estate appraiser, and experts in your collectibles to periodically reappraise your collections, etc.

How It Works

> Michael was a professional gemologist throughout his entire career. He and his spouse, Eliza, had prepared what appeared to them (and to their attorney) to be a rock-solid estate plan. Michael predeceased Eliza. Going through his belongings, she came upon a small lockbox containing dozens of cut gems ranging from diamonds and rubies to semi-precious stones. She knew instantly they had not re-titled them in their trust. Eliza went right away to her husband's go-to gem appraiser, documented and labeled each stone for type, value, and heir. Their estate attorney re-titled the gems and documentation to the trust along with the 'who gets what' list Eliza had drafted. Michael and Eliza's heirs will have no reason to squabble over the gems!

Asset Valuation Checklist

Eliza knew that whatever assets they didn't tell their attorney about couldn't be protected. Keep building your own inventory of assets so that you don't repeat Michael's mistake.

Go to your assets inventory; make appointments for updated appraisals or valuations as you re-title each item to the trust. Periodically reassess not only the valuations but also your actual asset inventory for accuracy.

- Real estate appraisals: Document them every 3 to 5 years (or at the time of renovations or when the market shifts significantly).
- Investment portfolio review: Check your quarterly statements to monitor performance and make adjustments in individual investments.
- Inventory/Insurance check-up: Review all insurance policies against your most current asset inventory, as, over time, we all tend to divest ourselves of assets and acquire new ones.
- Transparent records: Keep updated valuations, policy adjustments, and investment reports organized and accessible to your spouse/partner, your trustees, and (if you have kept them so informed) your beneficiaries. You have created an estate plan for clarity; don't file updates separately from your other trust and estate documents.

Digital Asset Management: Safeguarding Your Online Presence

This is going to be a very personal decision. You need to consider how digital our lives have become.

How It Works

> 94-year-old Ruth publishes her own novels on Kindle (and makes sales!). She talks to great-grandkids over FaceTime and her British friends over WhatsApp. She has an active Facebook account and has an online password manager because she also does online banking and much administrative business over the web. Why wouldn't she also store her estate documents online? Well, she does!

Some of your assets may be digital. Beyond bank accounts and investment portfolios, online assets might include social media accounts, digital media, cryptocurrencies, and intellectual property. These aren't just financial holdings; they are part of your legacy.

Without a plan, your digital assets could be lost, locked away, or mismanaged—and sometimes, your loved ones might have no legal right to access them. The good news is that with a little foresight, you can protect, organize, and pass down your digital estate just like your physical one.

What Digital Assets Do You Own?

Before protecting your digital assets, you need to know what they are. Besides any money-generating online businesses, consider:

- Financial accounts: Online banking, investment platforms, retirement funds, PayPal, Venmo, and similar accounts.

- Social media and online presence: Facebook, Instagram, LinkedIn, YouTube, and personal blog accounts. This is not about their monetary value. It's about what happens to these accounts when you pass away. You can decide, and your family can take care of them according to your wishes.

- Cryptocurrency and digital wallets: Bitcoin, Ethereum, NFTs—any assets stored in digital wallets.
- Subscription services and digital content: Cloud storage fees, online courses, streaming services, SaaS fees, monetized platforms.

How It Works

> Morrie's thriving YouTube channel generated revenue for many of his retirement years. His spouse Roberta's Amazon Kindle account has actively sold her self-published business books for her for years, generating a steady income for her late into her 70s. However, Morrie and Roberta had both failed to add their respective online businesses to their estate documents. They also didn't tell anyone how to even access them. When they passed away, their family knew about the activities they had, but had no access to their accounts or that revenue. In effect, by not noting at least a master password, the couple had locked up their respective digital assets—leaving them inaccessible. A simple inventory and documented access plan could have lifted them out of limbo for their heirs to manage and grow, or cash out and close.

Passwords Matter

To avoid this dilemma yourself, use a password/login manager: A secure tool like LastPass, 1Password, or Dashlane can store your credentials securely. Store the master password in your estate documents.

- Protect cryptocurrency keys: Digital wallets don't have password reset options—losing your private key means losing your assets. Ensure trusted individuals know where to find these keys.

Incorporate Digital Assets into Your Living Trust

Just like real estate or investments, your digital assets should be part of your estate plan. If you have these types of assets, I would suggest having legal counsel, as good professional advice can save your loved ones from confusion, delays, or locked accounts later.

- Digital assets: Add them to your asset inventory; re-title them to the trust.

- Appoint a digital executor: This person will handle online accounts, transfer digital holdings, and close unnecessary subscriptions. Some digital assets hold financial value, while others carry deep personal significance. Decide what should happen to each one—close or transfer them; give password access or not, etc.

How It Works

> Daniel had several informal online businesses earning a good income. He had never incorporated the businesses until doing some estate planning. He took the incorporation actions his estate attorney recommended to ensure ownership. He then added those digital assets to his trust, with clear transfer instructions.

Advanced Strategies for Asset Protection

You have worked hard to build your wealth. Now you know that a last will and testament must go through probate, does not protect from creditors, and can be vulnerable to lawsuits and disputes. Asset protection through a living trust should by now be your 'go-to' solution to avoid probate, transfer assets smoothly to your heirs, and secure their legacy—but should it?

Here are a few extra suggestions for keeping your assets—your estate—secure. Be sure to discuss each one with your attorney so that you can make the best decision.

Use Irrevocable Trusts for Stronger Protection

- Assets in an irrevocable trust are no longer legally yours, meaning creditors and lawsuits can't touch them. In exchange, you get rock-solid protection. High-net-worth individuals, those doing legacy planning, and those wanting to shield assets from future lawsuits could benefit from this form of trust—ask your attorney.

How It Works

> Suzanna placed $3 million into an irrevocable trust for her children. When she faced an unexpected legal dispute, those assets were untouchable. Her kids' inheritance was intact.

Use LLCs and Partnerships to Shield Assets

A Limited Liability Company (LLC) or partnership are business-protecting structure that can separate personal wealth from business liabilities. This includes digital, brick-and-mortar, service, and professional businesses, and investment real estate.

- If someone sues your business, only the business assets are at risk—not your personal estate. File articles of incorporation with your state and create an operating agreement outlining management roles.

How It Works

> John owned rental properties in his name. When a tenant filed a lawsuit, his personal assets were put at risk right alongside the real estate. If he had established an LLC to own the properties, only the business assets (the real estate itself) would have been exposed.

Plan Ahead

You can't just move assets at the last minute to avoid a lawsuit—courts look at such self-interested transfers as fraudulent and can undo them, leaving your assets unprotected anyway.

- '*Look-back periods*' used by the authorities are from two to five years. During those years, your asset is not protected; after that period, it is safe. Fund your trust with your assets early for best protection later.

- Plan for legal challenges by setting aside a legal defense fund.

If your estate is contested, legal battles can quickly drain resources.

- Regularly update your plan. Laws change, so keep your asset protection strategies up to date.

How It Works

> Matthew knew his kids. He predicted that his estate would face emotional inheritance disputes among his children. He made his estate plan as bulletproof and as clearly stated as he could with his attorney's guidance, yet still set funds aside for litigation to ensure that his trust could withstand challenges without draining resources.

Updating Your Trust: Keeping It Aligned With Life's Changes

Your estate plan should move with your life, with regular reviews and updates you make with your attorney. Getting any of this wrong (or just waiting too long to correct these items), there could be a lot at stake!

Reviews and updates are so key to effective estate planning because life happens. Keeping it current. It will take a couple of hours twice a year to sit with your attorney. Don't procrastinate. Life moves faster than we'd like. Update your trust documents in the following cases:

- Marriage, divorce, or remarriage.

- Birth or adoption of a child. Think about new educational funds and the need to appoint a guardian for this child.

- Major financial changes. You may inherit money, sell or buy a business, or make significant investments. In any of these cases, consider how newly acquired assets are protected and bequeathed, and remember to remove assets that are sold.

- Relocation to a different state. Estate laws vary from state to state. Moving across state lines may mean your trust no longer aligns with local legal requirements—an issue that can be resolved with a legal review.

- Changes in the law or tax regulations. Federal and state estate laws change periodically. A tax advantage that once benefited your trust may no longer apply. This makes periodic reviews with your attorney a vital need.

- Changes in trustee or beneficiary circumstances. Whether someone has died, or you've had a falling out (and many other reasons), you may need to appoint a new trustee or remove beneficiaries.

How It Works

Jax forgot to remove his ex-wife as a beneficiary in his trust. When he passed away, they'd been divorced for over a decade. Yet she was still legally entitled to much of his estate—a mistake Jax could have avoided with a simple update. What made it worse? He was married to someone else at the time of his passing. Jax's widow had a rude awakening!

How to Update Your Trust: Amendment vs. Restatement

In short, when any major life event occurs, your trust should reflect it—right away. A document written ten years ago likely doesn't match the realities of your life today, as Jax's loved ones learned the hard way. You have two options for modifying your revocable living trust:

- Amendments: This option is best for minor changes, such as adding a new beneficiary or updating a trustee. An amendment is a written legal document attached to the trust documents that changes specific sections of your trust while leaving the rest intact.
- Restatements: It may be easier (and cleaner) to create a trust restatement, which replaces the old trust while retaining its original start date for continuity.

How It Works

> Edward had already amended his trust five times over the years, which made it confusing and inconsistent. Rather than adding a sixth amendment, his attorney suggested that they simply rewrite the trust into a clear document. It was a complete update.

Keeping Trustees in the Loop

A trust isn't just an inert legal document—it's a living plan that involves real people. Keeping the interested parties informed by at least saying, "We updated our estate plan on May 15th this year," eliminates misunderstandings and may even help prevent disputes.

- If you change a trustee's responsibilities, let them know immediately. They need to be prepared to step in when the time comes.

How It Works

All Larry's children really knew about their father's plan was that he had one! They were shocked to learn that their inheritance was in a staggered distribution trust instead of a lump sum payout to each of them. They felt blindsided. However, the trust was rock-solid, and they had to accept their father's decision. They grumbled for a while, then came to see the advantage—particularly at tax time—of Larry's choice.

Catherine's trust was structured for maximum tax efficiency under old laws, but recent legislative changes in her state of residence rendered parts of it obsolete. She kept all her twice-yearly update appointments. Her attorney explained the new law; they adapted her documents so that she and especially her heirs could benefit from the new rules.

Chapter Six

Ensuring Compliance With State Laws—Keeping Your Trust Valid, No Matter Where Life Takes You

"The more informed we are, the more we understand and the better we're able to protect ourselves, our family, and assets."
– ***Spencer Sean***

Estate planning combines personal decisions with legal requirements that vary by state. Because estate and trust laws differ widely, working with a local attorney helps ensure your plan reflects current law and carries out your wishes as intended.

Your state of residence can also have a significant impact on estate taxes. Some states impose little to no estate or inheritance tax, while others do not. Understanding how your state treats wealth at death can help you plan more effectively, reduce unnecessary taxes, and, sometimes, factor location into long-term planning decisions.

Where Does Your State Stand?

Most states do not impose estate or inheritance taxes, but some ensure they cash in one last time. Where you live matters; a well-timed relocation before retirement could save your family thousands (or even millions) in taxes.

- No Estate or Inheritance Tax: If you live in Florida, Texas, Nevada, or most other states, your heirs won't face extra state taxes on what you leave behind.

- Estate Tax States: States like Oregon, Massachusetts, and Illinois impose estate taxes with lower exemption thresholds than the federal limit. This means you could owe state estate tax even if you're exempt federally.

- Inheritance Tax States: If you live in Iowa, Kentucky, Maryland, Nebraska, New Jersey, or Pennsylvania, your heirs might owe taxes on what they inherit—depending on their relationship to you. Spouses and children often receive a break, while distant relatives and non-family members pay the highest rates.

- Maryland's Double Trouble: Maryland is the only state that imposes both an estate tax and an inheritance tax—so if you live there, your heirs might need an accountant before they even see a penny.

How It Works

> Clarissa lives in Oregon, where the estate tax exemption is only $1 million. Her heirs would owe state estate tax on $2 million since her estate is worth $3 million. To reduce her taxable estate, Clarissa gifts the maximum allowed each year annually to each of her three children for the next 10 years, thus shrinking her taxable estate while helping her kids financially now.

Residency Matters: Are You Taxed in the Right State?

Think your state residency is obvious? Not so fast. States love to claim you as their taxpayer if there is any ambiguity. Your official residency is determined by the state where you spend the most time; the state where you vote, bank, and register your car; the state where you have your primary home.

How It Works

> Bob and Leah own homes in New York and Florida. If they spend 183 or more days in New York, they're considered New York residents, and New York has an estate tax. If they carefully spend more documented time in Florida (which has no estate tax), their heirs could avoid a massive tax bill.

If you own property in multiple states, make sure the state with the best tax laws claims you as its own.

Why State Laws Matter Beyond Taxation

- While the basic structure of a living trust is similar across the U.S., each state has its own set of rules regarding how that trust must be written (legal language and format), administered (trustee rules), and enforced. For instance, from state to state, the specific language in your documents can vary. The minimum age and residency status of a trustee can vary. In some states, out-of-state trustees must appoint a local representative. The information your beneficiaries may have—and the timing of its disclosure—can be determined by your state. In some locations, your trust must be notarized and/or signed in front of specific witnesses to be valid.

What happens if your trust is not state-compliant? The trust may be declared invalid—which means your estate could go through probate anyway. Your assets might not be distributed as intended, opening the door for family disputes or costly legal battles. Your beneficiaries could face delays, taxes, or reduced inheritances because of mistakes in the structure or execution of the trust.

Your legal residency determines which state laws govern your trust. If you move to another state, your new home may have different trust requirements, and your old trust may need revisions or a complete rewrite to be legal.

If you're married and living in a community property state (such as California, Texas, Arizona, or Washington), make sure you are consulting a local estate attorney because things can get complicated! Any assets acquired during the marriage are typically considered to be equally owned by both spouses, even if only one spouse is listed as the 'owner'. Also, transferring community property into a trust often requires mutual consent and careful legal documentation.

If you're in a community property state, work with an estate attorney familiar with local laws to avoid unintentionally invalidating parts of your trust. Surviving spouses or heirs may face disputes or unwanted tax consequences without proper planning.

How It Works

> In a community property state, Jessica placed her investment property into a trust without her husband's input. Because it was community property, the action was not valid, and the trust was challenged after her passing.

- If you move across state lines, book a review with a local estate attorney. In periodic reviews, make sure your trust is up-to-the-minute in all ways, including referencing current statutes and incorporating updated language based on the latest changes in the law.

How It Works

> Texas residents Tom and Elena have been married for over 30 years and built a comfortable life together, including a home, retirement accounts, an investment portfolio, and a multifamily rental property. Like many couples, they created a living trust to simplify asset distribution and avoid probate.
>
> Working with an attorney, Tom transferred marital assets into the trust under his name alone. Because Texas is a community property state, this required Elena's written consent, which was not obtained. As a result, the trust was challenged, delaying distribution and drawing part of the estate into court—creating the very probate complications the trust was meant to avoid.

Navigating Probate or Avoiding It?

Probate is the court-supervised process of validating and settling a person's estate after they pass away. It ensures that debts are paid, that wills are validated, and that whatever is left is distributed to the rightful heirs.

- If there is a will, probate confirms that it is legitimate and follows its instructions. If there is no will, state laws (called laws of intestacy) determine who gets what.

- While probate exists for good reasons—such as protecting heirs and creditors—it often comes with downsides. It can be time-consuming (taking months or even years). It can be costly, including legal fees, court costs, and executor commissions. It is public, meaning anyone can look up your estate details.

- Remember that if there is a properly drafted trust, it escapes probate entirely. We've said it: when you place assets into a living trust, those assets don't require probate because they are no longer legally owned by you, but by the trust. Upon your passing, your successor trustee distributes the assets directly to your beneficiaries. There are no court delays, public proceedings, or probate fees. Your estate remains private and efficient.

How It Works

> Sonya had two daughters and a living trust that held her home, bank accounts, and investments. When she passed away, her trustee distributed everything within weeks—without setting foot in probate court. Sonya's daughters could grieve and move forward without the legal red tape.

Not All Probate Is Created Equal

Here's where it gets tricky: probate isn't the same in every state. Some states simplify the process by following the Uniform Probate Code (UPC). Others, like California and Texas, have unique probate laws and procedures. Then there are the many states that offer a streamlined probate process reserved for small estates (usually under a certain dollar threshold).

How It Works

> We'll give you just two examples. 1) In Florida, estates valued under $75,000 may qualify for a simplified process called *summary administration*. 2) In California, anything valued over $184,500 (as of 2023) is subject to full probate unless it is in a trust.

Think about just the value of a single-family home in a major Florida or California city, and you see that almost everyone in those two states pays something to the taxman!

Probate Courts and Trustees

Your heirs go to probate court if you pass away with either only a will or with no estate documents at all—you know this by now.

Even if you have a trust, there may still be some involvement from the court, especially if the trust is challenged, or the court finds the language or intention unclear; if there is a dispute among beneficiaries; or if the trustee needs guidance or approval for certain actions.

In these cases, the probate court can step in to confirm the trust's validity; ensure the trustee is acting in good faith; resolve disputes; or provide oversight.

Remember that a trustee is a fiduciary—they have a legal duty to act in the beneficiaries' best interest and follow the trust's terms. If you are a trustee, your 'best practice' is to document all details, from account balances to distribution decisions to beneficiary issues. Being organized can save time and stress if the court requests records.

Work with a specialist called a 'probate attorney' and have him request streamlined options. Many states have affidavit procedures for transferring small assets without undergoing full probate. In some cases, you may be able to file for expedited review.

How It Works

> When Aaron's mother passed away, she didn't have a trust, but she had all her documents in order. By filing a '*small estate affidavit*' as allowed in their state (which is how the attorney could streamline the matter), Aaron avoided full probate and closed the estate within six weeks.

How to Find the Right Legal Help for Your Trust

Hands down, the number one way people find an attorney, a financial advisor, or a tax expert is through a friend or trusted acquaintance who is already their client. This is often the best way as well. The second most common way is through online research for a local attorney, followed by a quick background check on the State Bar association website. However, this may not give you enough background to make a good decision.

Your state's bar association acts as a matchmaking site for finding legal professionals, and they maintain up-to-date directories of licensed attorneys in your area, and you can search by specialty, just as you can with Google. Also, look for attorneys who are Board-certified in Estate Planning or who have memberships in organizations such as the National Association of Estate Planners & Councils (NAEPC). This usually shows deeper expertise.

A great estate planning attorney understands federal law and is well-versed in the unique characteristics of your state. Ask your attorney how often he or she handles trust work in your state. An experienced lawyer licensed to practice in your state will know what specific trust language or formalities your state requires (such as witness signatures or notarization); be familiar with state-specific tax rules, probate thresholds, and inheritance laws; advise you on how local courts interpret certain trust provisions—something you won't find in a generic online template.

You may or may not be sure if your state is a community property state or if common-law marriages are recognized for estate planning purposes. A local estate planning attorney can help ensure that both spouses' rights are protected and legally acknowledged.

How It Works

> Tina moved from Illinois to Arizona but didn't update her trust for six years. By the time she revisited it, much of her trust language needed modification under Arizona law. A quick restatement fixed it, but Tina kept thinking, "What if I had died with an invalid, outdated trust?" A proactive checkup could have prevented the scramble.

Don't let your once-robust trust inadvertently become obsolete. Laws shift, and tax codes evolve, you move to another state, etc. Stay one step ahead. While you could subscribe to legal bulletins through your estate planner or state bar, or join local estate planning groups or workshops in your area, the best way to stay up-to-the-minute is simply to do those periodic estate plan reviews with your attorney.

Most people outside the professions have no idea about estate law at the federal level, much less at the state level. Changes in state law might not make headlines, but they can significantly impact your estate plan. Your state's estate tax thresholds may rise or fall, meaning that more (or less) of your estate could be subject to tax. Trustee eligibility rules might change, affecting who can legally manage your trust. Documentation and administrative requirements may be updated, altering what records trustees must keep or submit to the court.

- Perhaps you think you're keeping up with changes through your online resources. While they can certainly report changes in your state's laws that affect your trust, *you might miss that local* broadcast, *and it's nothing a national nightly news program would announce*! As a secondary habit, make sure to stay in touch with your attorney through his firm's newsletters, workshops and presentations, or meetings.

How It Works

> In one state, new legislation raised the estate tax exemption—meaning that from the next tax year forward, instead of taxing all estates over $3 million as it did in the past (the threshold for exemption), estates valued at $5m or less would be exempt from estate tax. With Sue and Manuel's estate valued at $4m, the new law now means that (in this state), their estate is not subject to estate tax. It is under the $5m threshold and exempt from estate taxes.

However, in another state, lawmakers introduced a new bracket for trust income, leading to higher taxes on trust-held assets.

Some states introduce new tax brackets for trusts with high-income assets. Others (like Sue and Manuel's state) adjust estate tax exemption levels, raising or lowering the threshold. A few periodically re-clarify trustee duties and reporting requirements, especially for trusts holding real property or operating businesses.

One country, fifty + potential outcomes. (District of Columbia has its own rules too!)

Making Legal Amendments (The Right Way)

If a change in the law affects your trust, it's time to sit with your estate attorney and write a legal amendment. It should incorporate the new legal requirements without disrupting your original intentions. If multiple updates are needed, consider restating your trust, which allows you to revise the document while keeping its original creation date. Once the amendment is made, communicate it clearly to the trustees and beneficiaries. This prevents confusion and ensures everyone understands their rights and roles.

How It Works

> Nick revised his trust after a state tax law change to include the new gifting strategies and updated distribution rules. He informed his children of the changes, as he did with every modification. He knew his kids, and keeping them posted about how the trust was evolving to protect them worked for them all.

As long as we have politicians, we will have taxes, along with occasional changes in tax rates and rules. What does this mean for you? Your current trust may still be effective, but it may not function as efficiently as it could. A periodic review can reveal opportunities to improve efficiency, reduce taxes, or simplify administration.

A trust that is carefully written but never reviewed is like a compass that is never recalibrated. It may still point north, but not as precisely as it once did. By staying attentive and making adjustments when needed, you help ensure your estate plan continues to serve you and those you love in the way you intended.

Chapter Seven

Engaging With Professionals and Avoiding Common Mistakes

"A goal without a plan is just a wish." — ***Antoine de Saint-Exupéry***

We're all on a learning curve. That's the case for most people when it comes to this new activity called 'creating a living trust' or 'doing estate planning'.

We're unsure of 'how this works' or 'what we need to say or do' to interact with attorneys and other professionals. We're a little shaky about how to get their business taken care of.

Don't worry! So far, this book has given you lots of background knowledge. That will help you determine the next steps. Learn how to select and work effectively with estate planning professionals.

Use this chapter as a memory-jogging checklist. We've discussed these items in prior chapters, so go back if you need to review the topics! If you decide to hire professional help, this chapter will give you the basics of doing that.

Getting the Most From Your Estate Planning Meeting

Ask Questions—Even the Ones That Feel Basic

Ask! There's no such thing as a silly question, especially when your legacy is involved. Good attorneys speak the law fluently; you don't have to. Come prepared with a list of questions—big ones, small ones, and even those that feel obvious. Let's be clear here, if you go with legal counsel, you are paying for their service, and they should answer your questions, and you should be satisfied you understand what you are getting.

Ask about tax implications, how often to review your plan, or what happens to assets in other states. If something doesn't make sense, say so. A good attorney will explain it without making you feel silly.

Start With Your Why

Before you even set foot in that office or hop on a Zoom call, take a moment to get clear in your head about what you want your estate plan to achieve. What are your goals? What purpose must your trust fulfill? As you've read these pages, have your intentions shifted? This isn't just about taxes and paperwork. It's about your legacy. You deserve clarity for you and your heirs, and peace of mind for you all.

Continue to ask yourself these key questions: *Do you want to ensure your children are financially secure? Do you have a family business you hope will outlive you? Do you want to support a cause that means something to you? Do you need to set boundaries* about *how and when certain people receive their inheritance?*

Your Asset Inventory

This is the 'what gets protected or passed on' piece.

Your attorney can't protect what they don't know about, as we've seen in some of the ***How It Works*** stories. Come with as comprehensive a list of assets as you can. If you're uncertain about adding an asset to the trust, discuss the pros and cons with the attorney. As a rule of thumb, include it on the list (at least in the beginning) if it's worth something, financially or emotionally.

Asset Distribution

This is the 'who gets what' piece.

Go back to your asset inventory. Consider your family dynamics. Go back to potential non-profit or charitable missions you are passionate about. Get clear on that (and it may develop, as we've seen, and that's okay).

Continue to ask yourself these key questions:

Who do you want to inherit your assets? Are there conditions (age, milestones, specific needs) regarding how and when they will receive them? Do you want to leave anything to friends, charities, or organizations? Are there items of sentimental value that need to be handled carefully?

Don't Keep Family Dynamics a Secret

It may feel uncomfortable, but this is not the time to be discreet about family tension.

- NOTE: All conversations with your attorney are private and confidential. This is what they call 'The Attorney-Client Privilege'.

How It Works

> Gio and Amy had four children, and as they grew to adulthood, they stopped getting along. There always seemed to be some in-fighting going on. They shared this dilemma with the attorney, who asked more questions about the bequests they had in mind and so on, then proposed some solutions that would 'keep feathers from getting ruffled' among the siblings.

Your attorney needs to know if you expect disputes, jealousy, or confusion. Is there a strained relationship between siblings? Do you have a blended family with complex dynamics? Is someone financially irresponsible or struggling with addiction?

Don't hesitate to 'reveal' these dynamics to your estate attorney! These conversations are confidential and key to building a plan that works. Remember that attorneys cannot propose a trust solution for what you haven't told them!

Take Notes and Speak Up

Even the best consultations can feel like information overload. Bring a notebook or record the meeting (with permission). Write key terms, next steps, and names of documents to gather. Clarify instructions. If you're told to 'fund your trust', make sure you know exactly what that means. Speak up if something feels off or incomplete. You're not being difficult; you're being thorough.

Common Mistakes in Trust Creation: How to Avoid Them

Remember that in creating a will, a living trust, or any other legal document is not the sole job of your attorney. You have certain tasks to complete, and we have seen what they are.

Your attorney has certain aspects of the work he will do for you and with you to make your estate as bulletproof as possible. Do your part.

Here I am listing **six mistakes** that are, as they say, 'all on you' to prevent.

Creating a living trust is a wise step toward protecting your assets and securing your family's future, but it's not a foolproof shield unless it is done correctly. Even minor oversights can have significant consequences.

The good news? All the mistakes listed below are entirely avoidable, with a little awareness and some professional guidance.

Mistake 1: Not Funding the Trust

This is one of the most common and consequential mistakes people make with living trusts. Many assume the job is done once the trust document is signed. In reality, a trust does not control assets unless they are properly transferred into it.

- Your home still needs to be re-titled in the trust's name.

- Bank accounts and investment portfolios must be registered in the trust's name.
- Vehicles, business interests, and digital assets may also require formal transfer.

If assets aren't moved into the trust, they will probably go through probate anyway. And isn't probate exactly what you were trying to avoid?

Mistake 2: Leaving Out Important Provisions

Another common oversight is failing to plan for the what-ifs. A good trust doesn't just distribute assets; it also lays out how, when, and under what conditions that distribution occurs. Key provisions that are often missing include:

- Guidance on updating your trust during your lifetime, and on structuring distributions that balance flexibility with clear, efficient administration after your death.
- Guidelines for what happens if a beneficiary passes away or declines their inheritance.
- A clear succession plan for trustees if your original choice can no longer serve.

Without these details, your trust could end up being challenged or difficult to administer.

Mistake 3: Not Reviewing or Updating the Trust

Life changes—and so should your trust. If you've experienced any of the following, it's time to revisit your document:

- Marriage or divorce

- The birth or adoption of a child or grandchild
- A move to a new state
- A significant increase or decrease in wealth, purchase or sale of assets titled to the trust
- The death or incapacity of a trustee or beneficiary

Outdated documents can lead to unintended consequences, including assets going to the wrong people or tax benefits being lost.

Mistake 4: Failing to Communicate

Estate planning often involves sensitive decisions, and it can be tempting to keep everything private. But silence can cause problems. Consider at least informing your close family, "Your mother and I have an estate plan, and it was updated in June." Also consider sharing:

- Your intentions, especially if they might surprise or disappoint someone.
- Who is named as trustee, and what their role entail?
- Any updates or changes to the trust that affect others.

Clear communication helps prevent conflict, reduces confusion, and makes administration smoother.

Mistake 5: Doing It Alone Without Legal Review

You can go with DIY estate planning route. Seeking and following professional advice and getting expert reviews are still crucial. Laws are complex and change at the federal level while also varying from state to state. A poorly written trust can cause far more harm than good. Legal review matters so that attorneys can:

- Identify vague language or missing legal elements.
- Ensure the trust complies with current laws and your state's requirements.
- Align your trust with your other estate planning documents (like wills and powers of attorney).

Mistake 6: Ignoring Tax Implications

Poor planning can lead to missed tax savings or unexpected liabilities. Trusts, especially irrevocable ones, have their own tax rules—and without careful structuring, your estate or beneficiaries could pay more than necessary. To avoid this:

- Ask your attorney or tax advisor about tax-smart strategies for your specific assets. Does this mean a revocable trust is the right choice, or do you require an irrevocable one?
- Review potential inheritance, estate, and income tax exposure.
- Understand capital gains and the step-up in basis rules.

In a Nutshell

Work with a qualified estate planning attorney to get advice, professional drafts, and well-informed reviews of the elements of your plan and changes in your circumstances. Perform needed updates. Review your asset titles, registrations, and valuations carefully. Double-check at the time of re-titling that your financial institutions have processed it correctly. Consider learning and using estate planning software as a backup tool, not a replacement for legal advice. Revisit your trust every year (for those tax and estate law changes) or after major life events that occur in your life or the lives of your beneficiaries and trustees. Communicate openly with your trustees and (in relation to your family dynamics) your beneficiaries.

Vetting Professional Advice: Ensuring Accuracy and Relevance

Attorneys admit this: As trained and up-to-date as they believe themselves to be, they never expect to satisfy every prospective client that comes through their doors. Clients consulting other attorneys is understood; choosing a planner is a big decision. It's only good planning!

Choose a qualified advisor who fits your needs. You should be comfortable speaking with these advisors and meeting with them regularly.

If you are still in the market, so to speak, for an estate attorney, a tax specialist, or a financial investment advisor, do your research. Interview a couple of them. They are used to it and most, if not all, of them offer a free, no-obligation 30-minute consultation.

Here's how to proceed.

Verify Credentials

- Look up an attorney's credentials on the State Bar Association's online directory to ensure they're qualified and reputable.
- Look up their education (schools attended; years degrees

were awarded) and licensing to practice law; confirm they're licensed in your state through the state bar association; look for any disciplinary actions or professional complaints.

- Check if they are not only licensed but also specialize in estate planning or have relevant accreditations.
- Has the attorney published articles or a book on the subject that shows expertise?
- Read online reviews; are there testimonials from past clients on the law office website or review sites? Notice patterns in feedback—do clients say they felt heard, supported, and informed? Or confused and overlooked?

You're not just hiring expertise—you're entering a relationship. Trust and communication matter just as much as technical skill.

Evaluate the Relevance of the Advice

Even a well-qualified professional can give advice that doesn't quite fit. That doesn't make them wrong—it just means their suggestions might not align with your personal goals.

- Does the plan they've produced for you reflect your priorities, like reducing taxes or protecting vulnerable heirs?
- Is the strategy tailored to your family structure, business interests, or charitable goals?
- Are they considering the laws in your state, not just national best practices?
- Laws change—especially around tax exemptions and trust

rules; state-specific requirements can differ widely. A plan based on outdated laws could lead to penalties, invalid documents, or probate surprises.

Generic advice means your attorney isn't listening—a crucial skill. Find someone new.

Don't Be Afraid to Get a Second Opinion

- Not feeling heard may mean you need a different estate attorney; consult another estate planning professional to compare strategies.
- Ask for alternative approaches or new risk assessments.
- Use the second opinion to confirm or invalidate the first.

This isn't second-guessing. It's ensuring you feel fully informed before deciding about affecting your legacy.

- Once you've selected your attorney, schedule regular check-ins, even if nothing major seems to have changed. Attend their educational workshops or webinars. Have your lawyer inform you of key legal changes affecting your estate plan.
- Let me remind you that you are not creating your living trust and estate planning because you are minutes from retirement! Parents with young children create such plans, too, so that if anything should happen to one or both parents while the kids are still young, there are solutions in place. Likewise, single people of younger ages with some assets also consult estate attorneys to create protective plans.

- However, most who do this planning are in their fifties and thinking about retirement. Experienced estate attorneys often partner with tax professionals, healthcare planners, and financial advisors.

You can get solid legal support, protect your legacy, and still walk away with your wallet intact.

Many attorneys offer discounted package deals when you handle these multiple estate planning tasks at once. It's more efficient for the attorney, and that often translates into lower per-service costs for you. Instead of creating documents one by one, consider bundling:

- A will plus a living trust
- A healthcare directive (which is a power of attorney for medical decisions) plus a financial power of attorney
- Full estate plan packages (which may also include guardianship forms, HIPAA releases, investment planning, advice on ensuring income throughout retirement, tax mitigation or elimination in retirement, etc.).

Low-Cost Alternatives for Simple Needs

If your situation is straightforward with few assets to protect, there are affordable (and even free) options that won't have you in a high-priced attorney's office:

- Legal aid clinics: Many communities host free or low-cost legal clinics for those with limited incomes. These can help with document review, answering questions, or basic planning.

- State bar referral programs: Some state bar associations provide reduced-rate consultations through vetted attorneys.

- Do-it-yourself apps, software and other tools that are available over the internet (more on those in a coming chapter).

These tools are not substitute for tailored legal advice in complex cases. But for the basics, or to get started on a shoestring budget? They're a user-friendly start.

Prep Like a Pro to Minimize Fees

Your attorney's time is valuable—which means your preparation is a time- and money-saver for you, too. The more organized you are, the more you'll get from each billable hour.

- Write your goals and questions ahead of time. Bring a complete asset list: real estate, bank accounts, retirement funds, digital assets, and insurance policies—as well as prior estate documents if they exist.

Think through tricky family dynamics in advance—this will help your attorney craft the right language and strategies without requiring extra meetings to figure things out.

Set Expectations and Define the Scope of Work

A common reason estate planning costs increase is because of a lack of clarity. Avoid this by:

- outlining what you want done before work begins.

- asking your attorney to confirm the scope in writing.

- saying no to unnecessary add-ons if they don't serve your current goals.

A good estate plan develops. You don't have to solve everything in one go. Start with what's essential and expand as needed.

How It Works

> Jacob and Rebecca feared an estate attorney's services would cost 'an arm and a leg'. They finally just went for an exploratory appointment. They discussed costs upfront. They asked about flat rates and the attorney's hourly rate, and what services that covered. The attorney proactively took over that conversation with a detailed price sheet, information about payment plans and explained the contract they would sign. That transparency led the couple to use this attorney!

The actual goal is having a living trust, a will, and other estate planning documents that are legally valid, reflect your wishes, and fit your budget. By combining professional guidance with smart cost-saving strategies (and a little DIY), you'll feel confident in your decisions, maintain control over spending, and avoid costly mistakes in the future.

In the following chapter, we'll explore digital tools and resources that can support your estate-planning trek and keep you organized every step of the way.

Chapter Eight

Digital Tools to Draft Your Trust & Will

"*Death is not the end. There remains the litigation over the estate.*" — ***Ambrose Bierce***

We gave you some tips for working with an estate attorney in the last chapter. DIY'ers can find software tips for self-planning in this chapter.

Use online resources—and read this book—to educate yourself before consulting a trained attorney. Use the software to get a first draft of your trust information for your first meeting with the attorney.

This said, digital tools are getting more and more accurate (like AI for medical diagnoses). For trusts and wills, this is true: *Software and SaaS developers are trying to help you do-it-yourself for your estate plan.* Estate planning software, once expensive, is now publicly and affordably available online. Planning will clarify whether you need a lawyer, and to what extent.

How Artificial Intelligence Can and Cannot Help With Living Trusts	
What AI Tools Can Help With	**What AI Tools Cannot Do**
Organize personal information, asset lists, and account details	Provide state-specific legal advice
Explain basic living trust terms and concepts in plain language	Draft legally valid trust documents
Generate planning checklists and discussion questions	Replace an estate planning attorney
Help you think through goals, priorities, and family scenarios	Ensure compliance with changing state laws
Assist in preparing questions for an attorney meeting	Execute, notarize, or fund a trust
Summarize general estate planning options	Guarantee documents will hold up in court
Support education and early-stage planning	Address complex situations like blended families without professional review
Act as a planning assistant or organizational tool	Confirm tax treatment or asset protection strategies

1. Quicken WillMaker & Trust (2025)

Quicken WillMaker & Trust is the original estate planning software created by Nolo, featuring over 35 estate planning documents and updated annually by expert attorneys. The 2025 version includes significant interface improvements and new legal documents.

Key Features

- Comprehensive document creation: wills, living trusts, power of attorney, health care directives, transfer on death deeds
- 2025 improvements: streamlined interface, new forms including Authorization for Minor's Medical Treatment and Elder Care Agreement
- Available online or as downloadable software with document backup capabilities
- Interview-style process with legal manual and state-specific signing instructions

Pros

- Most comprehensive document library (35+ forms)
- Onetime purchase with no recurring fees
- Software vetted by qualified attorneys and covers a wide range of topics

- Works offline once downloaded
- Excellent for complex estate planning needs

Cons

- No attorney consultation option available
- Difficulty importing documents from previous versions - may require repurchasing annually for updates
- The interface can feel outdated and cluttered
- Not valid in Louisiana, U.S. territories, or Canada
- Learning curve for non-tech users

Best For

Individuals with comprehensive estate planning needs who prefer a one-time purchase and don't require attorney help.

2. LegalZoom

LegalZoom is one of the largest online legal services providers, trusted by over 2.1 million estate planning customers, offering comprehensive estate planning with optional attorney support. Options for a basic will and trust, couples packages and attorney consultations.

Key Features

- Complete estate planning bundles with will, trust, healthcare directives, power of attorney, HIPAA authorization

- Access to attorneys in all 50 states for consultation
- Documents reviewed by attorneys and accepted in all 50 states
- 60-day money-back guarantee if the company makes a mistake
- Step-by-step process that can be completed in 15 minutes

Pros

- Strong attorney support network with affordable consultation fees
- Comprehensive document packages
- Entirely online process with no software downloads required
- Well-established company with a proven track record
- State-specific legal advice available

Cons

- Higher pricing compared to some competitors
- Attorney consultations limited to new legal matters only
- Information provided isn't protected under the attorney-client privilege
- Customer service quality issues reported with long wait

times

- Charges for revisions after the initial period

Best For

Users who want comprehensive estate planning with professional attorney guidance and don't mind paying premium prices.

3. Rocket Lawyer

Rocket Lawyer is a robust estate planning tool offering various legal documents beyond estate planning, with the unique ability to work directly with attorneys.

Key Features

- Comprehensive estate planning documents: wills, trusts, power of attorney, living wills
- Direct attorney consultation via chat, email, or phone
- Living trusts that avoid probate and provide privacy
- High customer satisfaction with 4.7/5 stars on Trustpilot from 7,000+ reviews
- Templates include digital asset and property bequests

Pros

- Free document creation during the trial period

- Access to attorney consultations via multiple channels
- Wide range of legal services beyond estate planning
- Customers highlighted the free document feature and range of legal forms
- Modern, entirely online platform

Cons

- Expensive membership fees, especially when paying monthly
- Must maintain membership to make document changes after trial
- Limited estate planning scope - doesn't include home estates, trusts, medical planning in basic service
- The interface feels dated and challenging to navigate for estate planning newcomers

Best For

Users who need ongoing legal support across multiple areas and can justify the higher subscription costs.

4. Trust & Will

Trust & Will is a streamlined online estate planning service that has helped over 200,000 customers since 2017, focusing on user-friendly estate planning with excellent customer support. This has the option of adding in attorney support.

Key Features

- Four essential documents in the basic package are : will, living will, HIPAA authorization, power of attorney
- Unlimited document updates and secure digital storage
- State-specific documents with free shipping and notarization instructions
- 15-30 minute completion time with step-by-step guidance
- 30-day money-back guarantee

Pros

- Excellent customer support available before and after purchase
- Modern, user-friendly interface requiring no legal experience
- Affordable pricing starting at $199, significantly lower than traditional legal services
- Comprehensive plans cover all major estate planning needs
- Two-step verification for document security

Cons

- No option to purchase individual documents - only packages
- A $19/year membership is required for unlimited document updates
- Not ideal for complex family or financial situations
- Attorney help costs an additional $300

Best For

Seniors and individuals who want uncomplicated, at-home estate planning with excellent customer support.

5. GoodTrust

GoodTrust, founded in 2020 by Rikard Steiber, specializes in digital estate planning and offers comprehensive estate planning focusing uniquely on digital asset management.

Key Features

- All-in-one plan protecting physical and digital assets
- Unique "Digital Vault" for organizing online accounts and digital assets with lifetime access
- Average completion time: 20 minutes
- Documents valid in all 50 states with proper witnessing and

notarization

- Digital wills outlining digital presence management and asset transfer capabilities

Pros

- Innovative digital vault features for online asset management
- Competitive pricing with family plan inclusion
- Beautiful design and user interface with clear guidance
- Unlimited customer support available 7 days a week
- Addresses the growing need for digital asset protection

Cons

- No attorney support available
- Documents aren't state-specific (though valid with proper execution)
- Some user reports of platform limitations for complex trust structures
- Newer company with less track record than established competitors

Best For

Individuals with significant digital assets who want modern estate planning that addresses both physical and digital legacies.

The Online Estate Planning Revolution

For complex estates, these digital tools provide a clear, organized foundation to share with your attorney. For simple estates, these tools save time and money. You can now draft a will or create a trust from your couch. However, convenience comes with trade-offs.

The advantages of online estate planning are compelling. You can access these platforms anytime without scheduling appointments with advisors, and they cost a fraction of what attorneys charge. With typically two or three subscription price points, you pay only for what you use. Most programs provide comprehensive user tutorials to guide you through the process, and some offer ongoing subscriptions with continued access to legal help for questions that arise.

Yet users frequently encounter notable disadvantages. These platforms offer limited personalization and aren't designed to handle many complex situations that arise in estate planning. There's also the risk of legal gaps, as you may not know if attorneys helped create the software or how often they update it for changing laws. The software assumes everything you enter is correct and provides no call-outs for potential errors. Additionally, data security concerns persist, as some platforms don't clearly show their encryption or privacy protocols.

When choosing an online estate planning platform, look for a well-reviewed, positive reputation with ma verified subscribers; a state-specific document option; clarity on their security features (encryption, Two-Factor Authentication); and access to live customer and/or legal support.

A cloud-based plan puts your documents in an internet-accessible 'place' as long as you communicate the password(s) to those who count. Share all or parts of your estate plan with whomever you choose.

Templates and Form Builders

Templates you can download or complete online provide a starting point for revocable, irrevocable, family, or charitable trusts. Many can add clauses for minors, guardians, or donations. Form builders offer step-by-step guidance. They adjust the language based on your answers and generate documents in real-time.

While templates and form builders can be helpful, once again, be aware of state-by-state legal variations. Be aware that some providers have outdated templates (and often it's only an attorney who knows this). Be cautious because there may be invalid clauses or missing notarization requirements on your chosen template (again, an attorney will know this).

Two popular platforms that offer **updated, state-specific documents** (well-reviewed in mid-2025):

- Nolo.com
- US Legal Forms

Here are some links to resources for these tools for your research as you decide if this is the right path for you.

Quicken WillMaker & Trust (2025) NerdWallet. (n.d.) . *Quicken WillMaker review: Pros, cons and pricing*. Retrieved May 26, 2025, from https://www.nerdwallet.com/p/reviews/investing/estate-planning/quicken-willmaker

LegalZoom SeniorLiving.org. (n.d.). *LegalZoom estate planning review 2024*. Retrieved May 26, 2025, from https://www.seniorliving.org/finance/estate-planning/legalzoom/

Rocket Lawyer SmartAsset. (n.d.). *Rocket Lawyer review*. Retrieved May 26, 2025, from https://smartasset.com/estate-planning/rocket-lawyer-review

Trust & Will NerdWallet. (n.d.). *Trust & Will review: Pros, cons and pricing*. Retrieved May 26, 2025, from https://www.nerdwallet.com/p/reviews/investing/estate-planning/trust-and-will-review

GoodTrust NerdWallet. (n.d.). *GoodTrust estate planning review*. Retrieved May 26, 2025, from https://www.nerdwallet.com/article/investing/estate-planning/goodtrust

Chapter Nine

Maintaining and Updating Your Living Trust

"*Money-giving is a very good criterion . . . of a person's mental health. Generous people are rarely mentally ill people.*" —***Dr. Karl A. Menninger****, quoted in NEWSWEEK, November 2, 1959*

Your living trust and other estate documents are now written, either solely through consultations with an estate attorney and other advisors, or through a combination of DIY and attorney support. Keep in mind if you go it alone there is no one to hold accountable. Having a lawyer enhances the chances of legal compliance, but it also creates a potential source of reimbursement or damages for any serious errors in the trust.

Your documents should not be static, and we've said this repeatedly! Your living trust results from your life's milestones, relationships, and decisions. And as long as you are alive, change will be the only rule for how your life develops. Kids grow up and leave the nest. Finances stall, rise, and fall. People you trusted, well, they come and go from your life, or pass away. Keep your trust documents updated!

When It's Money that Changes

Your financial life might not be as stable as you thought when you first drew up your trust and estate documents. This is also a reason to adjust your trust. Do you have new assets that are properly titled in the trust? If you've sold other assets, remove them from the trust.

The Change Checklist

An annual review doesn't need to be complicated. Most attorneys provide all estate planning clients with an Update Checklist that prompts their memory.

List the following events that have occurred in the past three months:

- Any major life events for your beneficiaries such as marriage, birth, death, or divorce—or an out-of-state move for you?
- Changes in trustee status (current trustee, successor, and alternate trustees)?
- Bought, inherited, sold/donated any major assets that need to be added to or removed from the trust?
- Changes in your financial situation?

- Healthcare or end-of-life preferences to update?
- New/changed state or federal laws that affect your trust?

If you answer yes to any of these questions except the last one, it's time to meet with your estate planning attorney to make the updates.

Relationships come and go, sweeten and sour. Assets come and go. And laws can evolve so fast you suspect they were written in pencil in the first place! Don't let your trust sit untouched for years; it risks becoming outdated, inaccurate, or legally vulnerable.

The most common oversights attorneys see:

1. Beneficiary designations are not updated, even in the momentous case of births, deaths, marriages, divorces, or estrangements. Contact information is not updated.

2. Trustees reconsider (or you do, about them) and you don't name a new one, or not soon enough. While no beneficiary needs to know the details of your plan before your death, a trustee must. Contact information and old trustee designations are easy to miss but critical to fix.

3. No updates to your inventory of assets, or not quickly enough. You need to think not just about adding the asset to your inventory list, but about re-titling it to the trust.

4. Distribution instructions are outdated given the circumstances of the heirs. Perhaps you intended a sizeable lump-sum bequest for a young heir who has since turned to drugs; will that addiction lead the heir to burn through the money so quickly to feed the addiction that his health is further endangered? Consider such possibilities and realities at each review of your estate.

5. The family has not been fully informed or involved in your planning—now, with changes in your health or just with age, they need to be more informed. This serves to clarify your wishes while you're still here to explain them, prevent future misunderstandings or conflicts, and help your trustees and beneficiaries feel more prepared. This is an opportunity to tell them what they need to know upon your passing, as far as locating documents and professionals to explain them.

What Your Estate Attorney Will Do

Your attorney's role in your trust maintenance and updating is to stay informed of the law's evolution and to make sure you benefit from that knowledge.

Your attorney will inform you in a timely manner of changes in the legal landscape so that you can decide how to adapt your trust to changes in the law. This will keep your trust compliant and honored by the court. In your interest, but also the attorney's, he will make sure your trust remains legally compliant.

Here's how just two changes to the law might impact your trust:

- Estate and inheritance tax thresholds may change, altering how much your beneficiaries receive and how much the taxman gets.
- Trustee responsibilities or powers may be redefined by law, requiring safeguards or other changes in your trust documents.

If your trust isn't aligned with these updates, you could face increased tax liability, administrative challenges for your trustees, delays, or disputes in asset distribution. The very goals your trust was designed to achieve could be undermined simply because the law moved forward, but your plan didn't.

Court rulings that reinterpret existing laws can mean the difference between a seamless plan and a tangled mess. Your attorney will help you assess whether your trust needs an update; redraft outdated clauses or provisions for your review and approval; in cooperation with your tax expert and/or financial planner, take advantage of new tax-saving opportunities. Taking these measures means you avoid compliance issues and courtroom challenges before they arise.

How It Works

Jennifer and Rob's trust was established a decade ago in a state where inheritance taxes were relatively high. They structured their asset distribution to minimize tax exposure. Effective on the coming January 1st, their state has lowered its inheritance tax threshold. When they read this in the press, they sat with their attorney, who confirmed to them that their trust was no longer optimized for the new rules.

Jennifer and Rob decided on a re-appraisal of their high-value assets; discussed how to re-allocate them and shift more wealth into direct transfers to their heirs during their lifetimes; evaluated the benefits of creating one, perhaps two, new trusts. When discussing all this, the attorney confirmed that their choices simplified the administration and reduced their costs. They amended their trust.

A few years later, their trust was again adjusted to reallocate investment assets because they found themselves in a new tax bracket. That change saved the estate over six figures and ensured that even more of its legacy reached its intended beneficiaries.

They also now understand that trust law varies by state and in each state can be changed by new legislation; the language of all estate documents must be state- and legal-compliant.

Any single change might lead to a cascade of other adjustments to remain compliant, clear, and enforceable. Even attorney-drafted amendments could affect tax status, trustee duties, or asset protection clauses. You should look to the attorney to identify the cascade of other modifications that are not apparent to a DIY planner. Attorneys draft clear clauses and enforceable terms. They also ensure that your amendment aligns with the rest of your estate plan (will, power of attorney, healthcare directives, etc.).

When writing your amendment, clarity is a requirement. Your attorney will identify the section(s) of the original trust being amended; employ full legal names, legal designations, and exact asset descriptions; be specific about timelines, conditions, and roles.

How estate documents—your will, trusts, your powers of attorney—are created, worded, and also signed varies by state. You'll need to ask your attorney for your state's rules. Then? Comply!

- Once the amendment and any new estate documents are drafted, ensure they are legally valid:

- You, as grantor, sign the amendment. A trust in a couple's names is signed by both.

- All acting trustees should also sign, especially if roles are changing.

- A notary public must (usually; check your state's rules) witness the actual signing to confirm the identities and willingness of the signers to confirm that all signers acted voluntarily; to protect against future claims of fraud, duress, or misunderstanding; to cement the amendment's authenticity in a legal proceeding.

Without proper signatures, witnessing, and notarization, your documents may not hold up.

Every amendment adds a layer to your trust documentation, so keep new documents with the original ones. Come up with a labeling and dating system for clarity.

Law offices often provide clients with binders for secure document storage, including updates. It is a trace of the evolution of your wishes, as well as proof that your estate may change with new legislation and rules.

Legal compliance and record-keeping are one aspect of your good management of your estate—communication is the other. Here's who should be informed:

- Trustees who need to understand their updated responsibilities and carry them out confidently.
- Beneficiaries, if their share, conditions, or status have changed.
- Financial institutions, if an amendment affects ownership, account access, or asset distribution.

This matters because it prevents confusion, delays, and legal challenges later; it builds trust among those involved in your estate plan; it reduces the chance of emotional disputes that can arise from being surprised by a change.

Let me remind you that you don't have to go into any detail with any party, but the individuals directly impacted by the amendment should be made aware that you have an attorney-drafted estate plan.

Where Your Plan Stands So Far

We've spoken about the living trust and the various types and purposes available to you for your needs. You know trusts avoid probate. You know about the healthcare and financial powers of attorney. You understand that a will can be useful, but that it is always subject to probate. We've looked at a few issues surrounding estate and inheritance taxation.

If you own assets or live in multiple states, use a local attorney for estate planning.

You have learned a few ways of starting out DIY and how to keep your paper and digital documents both safe and accessible. We've discussed what kind of life changes should take you to your attorney's office to make updates on your documents.

Since relationships are often challenging, let's next go deeper into that set of decisions called 'designating beneficiaries' in the next chapter.

Chapter Ten

Choosing Beneficiaries—Balancing Heart, Legacy, and Harmony

"Estate planning is an important and everlasting gift you can give your family. And setting up a smooth inheritance isn't as hard as you might think." — ***Suze Orman***

We waited for all the other information provided before this chapter to inspire and inform you about your estate planning options, but we know you've been thinking all along about your beneficiary designations, and about the 'who gets what, when, and how' aspects of writing up your bequests.

Choosing beneficiaries isn't merely about dividing assets when you're gone; it's about honoring relationships, meeting genuine needs, and helping to preserve harmony long after you're gone.

Picture a future family gathering—laughter, shared stories, and generations connected by love and memory. That's the legacy many of us hope to leave: not just money but unity and belonging. The choices you make today—especially regarding who inherits what, how and when—can shape that future for better or worse.

The Heart of It All: Family

Every family has its rhythm, its closeness, and its distances. Some bonds are easy and warm, while others may ... let's just say it this way ... carry the weight of history, hurts, and hassles.

Recognizing these emotional landscapes (and landmines) is a key part of selecting your beneficiaries wisely. Ask yourself:

- Who relies on you emotionally or financially?
- Are there past rifts that could resurface when assets are decided or when they are distributed?
- Is there someone who might feel forgotten or someone whose inclusion could cause tension?
- What do *you* want to do?

You don't have to, and probably cannot, fix every relationship with your living trust and its bequests, but you can acknowledge the realities. You can plan in a way that promotes fairness, understanding, and clarity.

How It Works

> If two siblings have always had a strained relationship, naming one as your successor trustee over the other's inheritance could ignite conflict. Here, a neutral third-party trustee might be a wise choice. This is what Jayne and her husband Roy did. It had been a lifelong failure of theirs (which they accepted in the end) to get their two children to get along. A third-party trustee worked for everyone.

Weighing Financial Needs: Not All Support Looks the Same

Your beneficiaries may be in very different financial and health circumstances during your lifetime. You observe that some may thrive, while others may need more guidance or long-term help.

Consider who might need help with education, housing, or healthcare, and if you can provide it. You may wish to create lifetime resources for a dependent with special needs or a chronic illness. If there are grandchildren, think about whether you would like to support them through an educational fund or in other ways.

Drafting your estate plan to meet real needs isn't favoritism; it's compassion. A well-structured trust can ensure that needs are met without causing resentment or imbalance.

How It Works

> Theresa is a single parent of three adult children. She leaves equal inheritances to her three kids, but only after she has set aside additional resources in a separate special needs trust for her disabled grandchild. Her kids have all come to accept, from tests, exams, and current circumstances, that this disabled child will require lifelong care. Theresa's creation of the special needs trust takes a load of worry off her own child's shoulders, while it honors all her offspring.

The Role of Age and Maturity

Youth brings possibilities, but not always preparedness. Consider what kind of structure will set them up for success if your beneficiaries are minors or young adults. Options to consider include:

- Leaving inheritances in trust with *staggered distributions* (e.g., at ages 25, 30, and 35).
- Naming a *guardian or fiduciary* to manage the funds until that age arrives.
- Planning for and expecting the heir to *meet milestones*, perhaps around education or health achievements, to trigger specific payouts.

A thoughtful approach helps younger beneficiaries grow into their inheritance rather than feel overwhelmed by it. Even if your child is legally adult, the kid may not be financially or socially mature. You can provide for the child even as you plan for an inability to manage money.

How It Works

Stephanie and Ed's only child is a son who has never hung on to money for very long. Despite his claims of independence, he remains financially unstable. This led Stephanie and Ed to provide for him, but not with a lump sum bequest. They provided that their trust would only pay him small monthly amounts after their passing, but the bequest would be for life. This would provide enough to help but not be enough money for him to do nothing. It was calculated to be just enough to pay for rent and food in a pinch. It was a form of annuity their attorney suggested to them, and they (and their son) are happy with the arrangement.

Non-family beneficiaries

Beyond your family, include close friends, caregivers, or charitable causes in your estate plan. This can be a beautiful expression of your values and appreciation; however, it also requires just as much planning as for family members.

Be careful to identify non-family beneficiaries and give clear details about them and your bequest(s) to avoid confusion or legal challenges. Ensure that charities are properly named, including their tax ID numbers, and ask your attorney to get their IRS Letter of Determination and research their good standing first. Also, be aware of how state laws handle non-relative inheritances to individuals you wish to honor, as some may be taxed differently.

A properly drafted trust can prevent disputes about non-family bequests and make your intentions undeniable.

Communicating With Beneficiaries

Envision your family discussing your legacy and provision for them.

Estate planning isn't just about documents and distributions; it's about communication. Having open, honest conversations with your beneficiaries can be one of the process's most powerful, healing, and forward-thinking aspects. It can also be fraught with emotion.

Older generations might believe that they do not need to communicate their wishes to their younger generations. They hold things close to the vest, so to speak. Many families don't discuss finances with their kids, even when they're older.

While it is certainly true about matters of finance, this non-communication is true in health care matters and later-in-life decision making as well. No one wants to think about, much less talk about, the eventuality of their death!

Talk about these topics, however, can avoid misunderstandings, distrust, inter-family conflicts, arguments, and later legal disputes. Such emotions and argumentative exchanges drain emotional resources, challenge love and trust, and deplete financial resources when they go to court.

We encourage you to value your relationships and honor them with clear, honest communication about your wishes.

Open communication lets your family clearly understand both what you've planned and why. It gives everyone the full background for your choices, facilitating future conversations about your wishes. Sharing your plans provides reassurance and prevents future worry.

Do and Don't—the Conversation

- Choose a calm, private setting. Thus, not launching such conversations during a crisis about something else. Don't start talking about it at a rushed encounter with family. Don't start the conversation at any celebratory family gathering because those will always be about something else, too.

- Do set expectations early by letting everyone know that the purpose of the conversation is your estate planning arrangements. Don't pop this conversation with anyone out of the blue.

- Do expect the talks to provide clarity and news about your preparations. Tell your family this is not about judging or disputing your decisions. Don't let it be a negotiation.

- Do speak from the heart: explain your intentions and the values behind your decisions. Don't be hurtful in how you present this information.

- Do tell family you "have a little speech to make, and please don't interrupt me till I'm done." Don't refuse to answer their questions, but welcome questions. Remind all family (if this is your choice) that you will not be revealing individual bequests and such. Otherwise, do welcome even the difficult or emotional questions and answer truthfully.

- Do stay focused. Don't let your family get you off course with demands or rudeness until you have said what you have to say.

Open communication prevents future conflict, even without specifics.

How It Works

> Beth and Jeff told their children about their living trust and attorney. That was all they said. The children went along with it because, after all, Mom and Dad had never shared much about their personal affairs with them.

Bring Clarity

If you are more communicative than Beth and Jeff, here are three ways you can do things.

Family Meetings: You might schedule an annual or biannual family gathering to share any major changes or updates. It is a chance to confirm your vision and answer questions.

A Letter of Intent: Write a personal letter explaining your decisions and goals. These can be sent immediately or given to the recipient upon your passing. This allows you to include wishes that may not fit neatly into a legal document (such as family traditions you hope will be continued). This letter can serve as emotional guidance and moral clarity when you're no longer there to explain your choices.

Document Sharing: If you have led what could be called 'a transparent life'—one where you have had no secrets from close family—you may choose to provide one or more beneficiaries with copies of the trust or will, knowing that the trustee already has access the documents. Include contact information for your estate attorney (as Beth and Jeff did) or financial advisor.

Third-Party Facilitator: Estate attorneys are often a third-party presence in family meetings and 'the bearer of delicate news'. An estate attorney's role in these cases is more to guide the conversation, keep things on track, and ensure all voices are heard.

There is no secret about it. These conversations can be emotional. If you expect tension between siblings, that past conflicts over finances might surge up again, or resentment or misunderstanding about uneven inheritances might erupt, it may be wise to hold the meeting with a neutral third party.

Being open doesn't just reduce confusion. It builds something deeper. Openness shows that your plan wasn't made in a vacuum—it was considerate, and loving. It allows your beneficiaries to ask questions now rather than raise objections later. It helps people feel seen, even if they don't agree with every decision.

How It Works

> Mary and Steve have one child, who will receive a larger inheritance because of caregiving responsibilities. Their other child had expressed no willingness to help with caregiving; she even avoided it like the plague! While this was all quite clear in the family, Mary and Steve still explained things quietly and compassionately, while expressing their deep love for both of their children. The non-caregiving child reassured them she never expected a bequest from them upon their death and she would always be thankful for whatever they left her. She then turned to her sibling and, in tears, expressed gratitude that he would do the caregiving when she could not bring herself to do so.

There is no doubt: when beneficiaries understand *why*, they are less likely to feel slighted.

Any beneficiary might feel they are owed more based on birth order, caregiving efforts, need, or their personal concept of fairness. Try to be clear and let everyone know that this is not a negotiation, but how you have already proceeded. Explain your reasoning quietly. If it helps you (or them), write it up as a letter. As you explain in writing or face-to-face, summarize your thinking (financial need, past support, special responsibilities, etc.). State your decisions honestly, without apology, but with kindness. You can acknowledge emotions while sticking resolutely to your decisions.

Life changes not only for you but for your family, beneficiaries, your trustees, as well as charitable organizations that are part of your trust arrangements. Keep those conversations going with the interested parties, even if you are one of those people who likes to keep the details close to the vest.

Give Them a Realistic Hint

It should be clear by now: what you give matters—but how you communicate your bequest matters just as much. Conversations about inheritance can be emotionally charged, especially when expectations don't match reality. That's why managing beneficiary expectations is not just a good idea; it's vital to preserving harmony and honoring your legacy.

Many assumptions about inheritance stem from your silence or their speculation. You can replace guesswork with understanding by clearly defining what each beneficiary can expect to receive and even how. Not all of you will be at ease doing this, so an attorney will always leave it to your discretion how to proceed.

Share your estate's value, beneficiary allocations, and distribution terms.

When people don't know what to expect, they fill in the blanks—often with inaccurate or overly optimistic ideas. A clear explanation now can save your loved ones a great deal of confusion and conflict later.

Use Legal Structures to Set (and Enforce) Boundaries

Boundaries aren't just emotional; they're practical. The right trust provisions can guide behavior, set conditions, and protect beneficiaries from their inexperience or impulsiveness.

Remember the trust provisions we've discussed that might work for you? Consider age-based distributions (e.g., portions of an inheritance released at ages 25, 30, and 35); milestone-based distributions for goals such as completing a degree, holding a job, or remaining drug free; disinheritance clauses or reduced shares for behavior that is harmful or legally problematic. Trusts with these types of provisions should be done with legal counsel. There are many state and federal laws that might prevent your child from receiving other benefits if there is a trust in place with these types of caveats.

These provisions are about aligning your estate with your values and encouraging responsibility. This is one of the major powers of trusts over other estate planning tools, such as a transfer on death account or joint tenancy in real property. You can ensure the beneficiary has met certain conditions before receiving their share, or have it go elsewhere if they don't.

Prepare for Disagreements—Before They Happen

Even with good communication, emotions can run high, and conflict may still arise. That is why it is wise to include a dispute-resolution process in your trust. Options include naming a neutral mediator, requiring mediation or arbitration before court involvement, and clearly identifying decision-makers such as trustees or advisors.

When tensions are high, professional mediation can provide a neutral setting for concerns to be heard and resolved with far less emotional and financial cost than litigation. Some trusts also require arbitration for all disputes, helping keep conflicts private and out of public records. Because enforceable arbitration provisions can be complex, it is important to discuss these options with an attorney in your state.

Inheritances are financial, but they are also deeply emotional. Clear processes help your loved ones feel respected, treated fairly, and supported during an already difficult time.

How It Works

> Lana's husband, Theodore, never shared details about their business interests or accumulated wealth with their four children. Lana respected his wishes. After his death, the children were unsure what to expect, so Lana met with them at the attorney's office to explain Theodore's intentions. When the attorney revealed the scope of the estate and each child's bequest, the children were surprised and emotional, coming to understand that their father's decisions had always been made with their best interests in mind.

Sometimes you just have to communicate in how you know works for your family.

How to Change Beneficiary Designations

We've said it and said it: Life is nothing but change. Life changes us, and also the people we care about. When change happens, you must keep your beneficiary designations current to maintain the integrity of your plan and communicate your appreciation to those you care about.

You need to *'amend'* your trust for these changes to take effect. Ideally, you should have an attorney help you take the following steps with an attorney at best so that all state laws are followed and required forms and language are used to update your beneficiary designations.

Draft a trust amendment: Use the correct language to state who is being added, removed, or changed. Always use the beneficiary's full legal name and birth date for clarity. Detail the conditions attached to the inheritance, such as age requirements, educational or health milestones to reach, etc.

Have the amendment notarized; notarization strengthens the amendment's legal standing and protects against future disputes. All required parties (e.g., grantor and trustees) should sign in the presence of a notary.

Revise related estate documents: Revise all new information across all estate documents, remembering life insurance policies, retirement accounts, and Payable-On-Death (POD) and Transfer-On-Death (TOD) accounts. Double-check everything with your advisor to avoid having conflicting designations. You don't want to delay or complicate distribution because you didn't double-check.

Notify trustees and advisors; inform them of the updates so they all have current information.

Amendments won't only be necessary for beneficiary designations. Laws can change how much your beneficiaries receive or how much they owe, as well as change estate thresholds. We've seen how that can cause an estate to owe much more in taxes, and that is money your heirs will never have. Likewise, other laws may enact regulations that may require revisions to trust structures or wording to remain in compliance.

Keep up with personal and legal changes that call for an amended trust. Use your review meetings to inform your attorney of changes you wish to make and ensure they are made correctly and in a timely manner. Honor your current and your lifelong relationships by keeping your trust up to date with intention, clarity, and love.

Chapter Eleven

Exploring Advanced Trust Options

"If it is not written down, it does not exist." — ***Philippe Kruchten***

Advanced trust planning can create a long-lasting, intentional legacy that shares with others not just what you've earned, but *who you are*. At this point, if you are reading this chapter, you have engaged a competent estate attorney, and the only DIY work you've done is prepping yourself with a good understanding of the documents and process through sources like this book.

Many types of trusts can take you beyond the basics, and we have already mentioned a handful of them: special needs trusts, irrevocable life insurance trusts, grantor kept annuity trusts, irrevocable dynasty trusts, etc.

From choosing between revocable and irrevocable trusts to establishing more specialized trusts for philanthropic giving, more asset protection, or unique legacy building, these trusts and other strategies we'll present now are designed to help you achieve your goals. The trusts need to be set up with care in language and form, so consult with your estate attorney for these choices.

Revocable vs. Irrevocable Trusts: Finding the Right Fit

Revocable Trusts (Living Trusts)

Revocable trusts are a natural first step in trust-based planning. They offer control, they can be modified or amended, and they are reasonably easy to set up and explain to others.

Advantages of the revocable living trust:

- You can change the language or assets in the trust at will and even dissolve the trust during your lifetime.
- It avoids probate, ensuring faster and more private asset distribution.
- It allows you to manage assets yourself or name a trustee to step in if you become incapacitated.

Disadvantages of the revocable living trust:

- Assets remain part of your taxable estate; that is, this form of trust is not as tax-efficient as you might wish.
- It offers no protection from creditors or legal claims, which you might discover too late.

Revocable living trusts are best for families just starting out, those wanting flexibility, or anyone who values ease of management during their lifetime.

Irrevocable Trusts

These trusts require a stronger commitment—you relinquish control over the assets—but they offer powerful advantages.

- *Advantages of the irrevocable living trust:*
- They remove assets from your taxable estate, potentially reducing estate tax.
- They shield assets from creditors, lawsuits, and financial risks since the trust owns the assets and not you.
- They can be structured to provide long-term wealth management across generations.
- They are great for high-net-worth individuals, those in high-risk professions, or families looking to preserve wealth long-term and minimize taxes.
- *Disadvantages of the irrevocable living trust:*
- They cannot be easily altered (or at all) without beneficiary consent.
- They are more complex and expensive to establish and administer.
- These are probably not the best option for a very young person, or for anyone with few assets.

To determine the trust structure that best matches your goals, ask:

- Do I want to keep control, or am I ready to give it up in exchange for stronger asset and creditor/lawsuit protection?
- Does my tax situation make mitigation a top priority?

Specialized Trusts for Advanced Planning

Once you've chosen a basic structure, discuss specialized trusts with your estate attorney, who can customize your estate plan and help you achieve very specific or much longer-term objectives.

Let's look at just four types of trust for now. They variously help you do charitable giving even after your death, protect your assets more completely, protect one or more of your chosen beneficiaries from themselves, and protect your residence for heirs, while also protecting your right to live in it for the rest of your life.

Charitable Remainder Trust (CRT)

- This trust owns an asset you have re-titled into the trust. The asset is a revenue-generating one, such as a piece of real estate. The trust pays you or your designated beneficiary the income it generates for a set term. When you pass away or when the term has expired, even during your lifetime, the asset goes to a named charity, which is henceforth the rightful owner. This trust offers you income for the term. It provides immediate income tax deductions and defers capital gains taxes on appreciated assets. This CRT is ideal for those who want to support a cause while benefiting from the income.
- The disadvantage? The term cannot be changed. If you des-

ignate a term of twenty years, but live thirty-two more years after setting up the CRT, you no longer have that income for your final twelve years.

Asset Protection Trusts: Guarding Your Wealth

Used to insulate assets from lawsuits, creditors, and claims, these trusts are often set up in jurisdictions with strong asset protection laws (like the Cook Islands or Nevada). The key benefits of these are that they shield assets from liability, offer greater privacy, and maintain long-term wealth stability.

> **Why Privacy Matters**
> One of the most overlooked benefits of a trust is privacy. Unlike a will, which typically becomes part of the public record during probate, a properly structured trust allows your assets, values, and distribution instructions to remain private—avoiding a court process that can require your finances to be catalogued and disclosed. For many families, this added discretion and control is a key reason to choose a trust over a will or intestate succession.

Note that these trusts must be established before a threat arises. You cannot use them to hide assets after a lawsuit has been filed. This said, the asset protection trust is ideal for physicians, business owners, and anyone exposed to legal or financial risk.

Spendthrift Trusts: Protecting the Beneficiary From Themselves

Designed to help beneficiaries who might mismanage a lump-sum inheritance, it is the trustee who controls distributions, releasing funds on a schedule or as needed. Creditors cannot access the trust's principal, and the trust ensures long-term support to the beneficiary as opposed to allowing massive, short-term spending. This trust is great for beneficiaries struggling with addiction, poor financial literacy, or a history of overspending.

Qualified Personal Residence Trust (QPRT): Minimizing Estate Taxes

This trust allows you to transfer your home to heirs at a reduced gift tax value while continuing to live in it. You retain the right to live in the house for a set number of years. After that term, the property passes to your beneficiaries. If you outlive the term, the home is not included in your estate for tax. This trust is ideal for homeowners with high-value properties who want to reduce their taxable estate.

Wills and Trusts in Harmony

We've presented the concept of a will (aka a Last Will and Testament), powers of attorney (POAs) for healthcare and financial matters, and you probably know people who only have these documents with no living trust as part of their estate planning.

When you combine trusts, wills, and POAs properly, they create a sound plan, documenting your ultimate wishes.

The Role of a Pour-Over Will

While a trust can hold and manage a significant portion of your assets, it may not cover everything. You may acquire a new asset or have forgotten to transfer a current asset into your trust—we've seen that in some of our stories. There is a safety mechanism for that.

Use a 'pour-over will' to achieve that. This is the name of the type of will that works in combination with your trust. The name is descriptive: This will is designed to 'pour over' any forgotten or newly acquired assets into your trust upon your passing. A correctly drafted pour-over will typically encompasses 'all assets not already in the trust' and not just assets specifically listed in the will. This means any assets you own at death that aren't already in your trust or otherwise designated to a beneficiary will be caught by the will and directed into the trust.

NOTE: A pour-over will take you to probate court. However, if you have an effective trust, it is only those assets not covered by your trust document that will be subject to probate. Also note that, unlike the Last Will and Testament, this pour-over will is not a standalone document but is created to work in combination with your trust.

It is smart to have such a pour-over will as a safety net, to catch any assets you forgot to transfer into the trust or for which you didn't get around to completing the transfer. It prevents those assets from being distributed according to the default state laws of intestacy. The pour-over will ensures that all assets—whether or not titled in the trust—are ultimately governed by the terms of your trust.

How It Works

> Thomas and Rebecca purchased a piece of land late in life but forgot to title it to their trust. Their pour-over will is going to capture that asset and ensure it ends up where it belongs—in their trust, to be distributed according to their wishes.

Confusion and disputes can result when the statements of the trust and the will don't match. That's why coordination is a must. Check your beneficiaries to ensure that your will and trust do not name different individuals for the same asset when that is not your intention. Beware, too, if you have created guardianship and healthcare directives, since they both typically belong not in the trust but in your will.

How It Works

> Dan and Lisa created and funded a family (living) trust. They had a modest estate, but it included a mix of real estate, retirement accounts, and other personal property of some value. They created their trust for their major assets and a pour-over will to capture everything else. When they pass away, the pour-over will is going to direct any overlooked assets into the trust, allowing for a smooth, *probate-free* transition to their children. Their documents were clear, consistent, and comprehensive. Their heirs had no court delays; there were no family disputes or confusion.

High-net-worth bachelor Nathan had, notably, an extensive, valuable art collection. While his trust managed his financial assets and property, the art remained in his name. A pour-over will was used to transfer the collection into his trust upon his passing, ensuring it would be preserved and distributed to the beneficiaries he designated, in exactly the manner he outlined. This dual approach allowed Nathan to enjoy his art collection during his lifetime, while protecting it for his heirs.

Three Trusts for Strategic Tax Planning

To maximize the efficiency of your trust—not to mention maximizing the protections it offers—often means minimizing or eliminating taxes for your heirs. You want them to get what you leave, and not just what Uncle Sam leaves them after taking his cut, right?

A trust that performs well financially also needs to perform well fiscally. And that starts with tax-aware structuring. Several types of trusts help you achieve tax efficiency, but you accept that this is really where your DIY stops: This is a very advanced trust law, indeed, and to benefit from the full power of the structure, you have to draft it, fund it, and manage it correctly.

Important Note on Legal and Tax Guidance

The information in the following section is provided for **educational purposes only** and is not legal or tax advice. Trusts used for strategic tax planning involve complex, highly state-specific and federal rules, and their suitability depends on your individual circumstances. Your estate planning attorney and tax advisor can explain whether these structures are appropriate for you, how they must be drafted and funded, and how they should be maintained over time to comply with the law and achieve their intended results.

Grantor Retained Annuity Trusts (GRATs)

Let's say a business owner expects the value of the company he owns to rise sharply. He can lock in future gains for his children/heirs with minimal tax exposure by placing it in a '*grantor retained annuity trust*' or GRAT.

- A GRAT allows you to transfer appreciating assets to heirs with little or no gift tax. You retain an annuity payment for a set term. If the assets appreciate beyond the IRS interest rate, the excess passes to beneficiaries tax-free.

Intentionally Defective Grantor Trusts (IDGTs)

With this strategy, a high-net-worth individual transfers *appreciating* assets to an IDGT, freezing their estate's value while accelerating wealth to the next generation.

- The trust is said to be '*defective*' for income tax purposes, meaning the grantor pays the tax. However, it's '*effective*' for estate purposes, removing appreciation from the estate. This trust allows asset growth to accumulate in the trust tax-free to beneficiaries.

Whatever type of trust you and your attorney believe will work best for you, the contents of your trust are just as important as the container itself. To maximize returns and reduce risk, diversify with intention. The following are key strategies:

- Align asset classes (stocks, bonds, real estate, and alternatives) with the trust's time horizon and beneficiaries' needs.

- Rebalance regularly to stay in sync with market conditions.

- Consider professional portfolio management tailored to fiduciary rules and long-term growth.

Some assets (like retirement accounts) have tax advantages that may not play well in certain trusts—a coordinated financial strategy is essential, so get your financial advisor in the room with your attorney and you.

Irrevocable Dynasty Trusts: Multigenerational Legacy Building

Dynasty trusts are of the irrevocable type, so you'll want the expertise of all your advisors to create it. These trusts allow you to think beyond your lifetime, establishing a legacy that lives on in both form and function.

In a nutshell, an '*irrevocable dynasty trust*' allows you to pass wealth down through generations without repeated estate or gift taxes. With these trusts, you take advantage of the *Generation-Skipping Transfer Tax* (GSTT) exemption. The trust has a long-term (even perpetual) duration, depending on the jurisdiction. There is robust asset protection for future generations.

A dynasty trust might hold investment/income-generating real estate to pass income and equity to grandchildren, great-grandchildren, and beyond. Taxes won't erode your asset value at each level.

Beyond the Trustee: Your Trust Protector

Here, you have yet another trusted individual to identify and name.

A '*Trust Protector*' is not a type of trust, but a person acting in the trust's interest—literally 'protecting' it from certain types of events or people. It is a different individual from the trustee, and you write the role of this person into your trust document.

Naming such a protector ensures flexibility in the rigid framework of an irrevocable trust. Trusts are often designed to last for decades, but life, laws, and families change. That's where a trust protector comes in. They can change trust terms to reflect legal or personal changes, replace trustees if needed, resolve disputes between beneficiaries or other parties, interpret unclear provisions, approve or veto distribution decisions in complex scenarios.

If your trust is irrevocable or multigenerational, a trust protector ensures it remains aligned with your original intent, even as circumstances change.

International Trust Planning

Trust planning becomes more intricate for individuals with international assets, beneficiaries, or business interests, and that group includes a lot of families. There are some challenges to consider.

- If we've discussed differing estate and tax laws and rules across U.S. states, the variations intensify across countries. You run the risk of double taxation. You must comply with reporting requirements under the Foreign Account Tax Compliance Act (FATCA) and the Common Reporting Standard (CRS) regulations. Note that the legal recognition of trusts varies by jurisdiction.

Solutions to those challenges may be to work with internationally qualified legal counsel, financial management, and international tax advisors. You might consider offshore or dual-compliant trusts in stable jurisdictions. Understand and use tax treaties and structuring tools to reduce friction and liability.

As you can see, this is quite an advanced trust and tax law! A U.S. citizen with property in Europe and adult children abroad can, however, set up an international trust structure to manage assets, avoid probate, and reduce taxation in all countries. Make sure to have your advisors explain what the rules and requirements are in plain enough language for you to grasp, it's in your interest!

Chapter Twelve

Planning for the Future

"Do the best you can until you know better. Then when you know better, do better." — ***Maya Angelou***

Legacy planning is far more than merely distributing wealth. It captures the essence of who you are—what you believe in, what you have worked toward, and the impact you wish to leave behind.

As you build an estate plan starting with your living trust, you'll notice something important: the heart and soul of your legacy lies in your values. You'll notice that principles have consistently guided your decisions. You've thought hard about what you wish for your children or loved ones to have learned through how you've lived your life.

- What does a life well-lived look like?

For some, it's about kindness, service, or faith. For others, it's about entrepreneurship, education, or artistic expression. There's no right answer—only your answer. When you define your values clearly, you provide future generations with a compass they can carry long after you're gone.

Your legacy isn't just about what you leave; it's about the steps you took to get there. Your personal history holds a powerful place in that story. Preserve it by sharing family stories and traditions—write them down or record them in your own voice. Include a legacy letter in your estate documents that expresses your hopes, dreams, and life lessons. Preserve photos, recipes, or cultural traditions that tell your story beyond monetary value.

Imagine your great-grandchild listening to a recording where you discuss your first job or the values your parents instilled in you. That emotional connection also becomes part of their story.

Once your values are clear, consider how your estate plan can serve them. Think beyond financial gifts; think in terms of impact. Consider these examples:

- Want to promote education? Establish a scholarship or education trust. Ask your attorney to explain the types of trust and the structure called a '*foundation*' that can achieve that.

- Want to encourage family connections? Fund annual family reunions or create a trust that supports travel.

- Want to support a cause? Use a charitable trust to fund it.

Set measurable goals tied to these intentions, such as "Fund three scholarships per year" or "Preserve and digitize 100 years of family photos." Your money tells your story when your trust documents and financial plans reflect these goals.

Philanthropy Through Trusts: Leaving a Charitable Legacy

Imagine that your legacy stretches beyond family lines—into classrooms, hospitals, environmental efforts, or communities you have never met but deeply care about. Through philanthropy in your estate planning, you can create a lasting impact that reflects your values and continues to serve others long after you are gone.

Charitable giving through trusts is not just generous; it is strategic. It can provide tax benefits, income opportunities, and the assurance that your wealth will support important causes. This chapter explores how to align your financial legacy with your values, structure your giving, and ensure that your generosity creates enduring change.

Choosing the Right Charitable Beneficiaries

Remember that we discussed the charitable remainder trust (CRT)? We did not discuss the charity that you'd name as your beneficiary—that's up to you. To guide your selection, identify missions or causes that resonate with your core values. It might be missions of education, health, the arts, the environment, social justice, or something else entirely.

Go online to read about potential charities through platforms like Charity Navigator, Candid GuideStar, or the BBB Wise Giving Alliance. Look for registered (with the IRS as a tax-exempt charity) organizations with a mission aligned with your values that are making a measurable impact in the community. Also, expect strong governance, financial health, and transparency. If you believe you are going to make a sizeable bequest to the organization, make an appointment to visit it if you don't already know it well and chat with the Executive Director.

Structuring Charitable Giving in Your Trust

- If you've already talked about charitable bequests with your estate attorney, you'll have learned how to structure them.

You might designate specific assets or percentages of your estate for charitable causes, include contingency plans in case a chosen charity ceases to operate, and consider setting up conditions for disbursement, such as requiring funds to be used for a particular program or scholarship, setting milestones (e.g., only release funds when matched by other donors), tying donations to community service or academic achievement.

- As a reminder, two commonly used trusts for this purpose are the charitable remainder trust (CRT) and the donor-advised fund (DAF). There is also the '*charitable lead trust*' (CLT), an irrevocable trust designed to provide financial support to one or more charities for a predetermined term. When the term expires, the remaining assets are distributed to (non-charitable) beneficiaries, such as family members or other loved ones.

- Each of these trusts has different rules, so make sure to go over each option with your estate attorney to choose the one that suits your circumstances and your wishes.

Behind every charitable trust is a story. And behind every gift, a life is touched.

How It Works

> The Martinez family created a CRT to support education initiatives in underserved communities. Their trust paid them income during retirement, since they funded the trust with income-producing real estate. Then, ultimately, they funded a scholarship program for first-generation college students. And enabled dozens of young people to pursue degrees and careers they once thought were out of reach.

One student, in a thank-you letter, wrote to them, "Your support didn't just help me financially. It told me that someone believed in my future, which changed everything."

Charitable giving through trusts transforms philanthropy into a long-lasting expression of your identity and your passions. You give with intention, support causes you care deeply about, and remind future generations that what matters to one person can help many in a ripple effect called 'paying it forward'.

Shifting Gears

Just as your life has shifted over time, so too will the needs and dynamics of your family. A good legacy plan leaves room for new grandchildren, changes in health, evolving priorities, and shifting economic or legal landscapes. Work with your estate planner to ensure that your trust documents include provisions for amendments or updates so that your legacy remains alive and not locked in the past.

Remember that your trust can be amended as needed to reflect changes in family structure, charitable goals, or values important to you, the grantor.

Imagine the day your children or your grandchildren step into the legacy you have carefully prepared them for. They are not just inheriting wealth or property, but something far more personal: your values, wisdom, and the legacy you have worked so hard to shape.

However, no matter how well-structured your plan may be, a legacy needs more than good intentions to endure. It requires people who are prepared.

With that in mind, let's explore a bit of how to equip your heirs with the knowledge, confidence, and sense of purpose they will need to carry your vision forward.

Financial Education: The Foundation of Stewardship

Have you heard that three-generation curse? It goes like this: *"The first generation makes all the money, the second generation manages all the money, and the third generation spends all the money."*

You are (presumably!) the first generation. Now it's time to make sure the second generation understands money management, and that the third generation coming up understands money management means more than how to spend it!

When it comes to preparing your heirs, financial literacy is as non-negotiable as a solid general education. Inheriting assets without the tools to manage them can do more harm than good. That's why education should begin long before a formal transfer occurs.

Multi-generational wealthy families educate their children very early about money, by teaching them how much ordinary and extraordinary purchases cost, about how much the average person earns in a week or a year, about saving money, budgets, and the difference between wants and needs.

Chances are, your family has not done that. So what can you do? Here are some ideas.

Financial Literacy at Any Age

Host family financial training workshops with an experienced finance professional. Bring everyone together—young and old—for engaging, age-appropriate discussions. Invite financial advisors, estate planners, or tax professionals to speak. Cover topics like budgeting, investing, trust administration, and philanthropy. Make space for questions, concerns, and real-life scenarios. The goal is education, not pressure.

Supplement those workshops with resources. Share books or podcasts that explain money management in relatable terms. Enroll the whole family in online courses or webinars on financial planning and wealth responsibility. Encourage them to set personal financial goals that align with your family's legacy vision.

Mentorship bridges experience and aspiration. While formal education is powerful, learning from real-life experiences is transformative.

Establish family mentorship channels by pairing younger heirs with elder family members or trusted advisors. Encourage regular check-ins to discuss financial decisions, career paths, and personal values. Create a safe space for learning, where mistakes are viewed as lessons, not failures. Offer shadowing opportunities. Invite heirs to observe trustee meetings or take part in legacy discussions. Let them sit in on annual reviews of trust performance or philanthropic strategy. Give them a seat at the table—literally—so they can understand the nuances of stewardship.

Sharing the Why Behind the What

Your estate plan doesn't just say *what* happens—it can and should tell a story about *why*. And when your heirs understand that story, they're far more likely to protect and honor it.

Hold regular family legacy meetings. Discuss your goals, values, and the intention behind your estate plan. Clarify the roles and expectations for trustees, beneficiaries, and advisors. Address concerns before they become conflicts. Share hopes for how the family can grow, give, and lead in the future. These meetings don't have to be formal. A weekend retreat or annual family dinner can serve as the perfect backdrop for heartfelt conversations.

Set up a secure, shared digital workspace for your family's legacy planning. Include trust documents, vision statements, meeting notes, and updates. Keep communication flowing across generations and time zones.

Include heirs in decision-making (the wealthy do this as part of their children's financial education). People protect what they help create. Involving your heirs in meaningful decisions invites them to take personal ownership of the legacy you've built. Ask for their input when amending trust provisions or exploring new family investments. Involve them in charitable giving—let them nominate causes or vote on donations. Assign them specific roles in family initiatives (e.g., event planning, communications, impact reporting). A family foundation invites teens to lead a 'next-gen giving circle', allowing them to fund causes they care about while learning the mechanics of grant making and accountability.

This active participation teaches responsibility and deepens their connection to the purpose behind the plan.

Finalizing Your Estate Plan

Completing your estate plan is not just the conclusion of a legal process. It is a profound expression of love, responsibility, and vision. Every piece of your estate plan is aligned, intentional, and strategic. A well-prepared estate plan doesn't just protect your assets; it becomes a legacy of clarity, compassion, and continuity.

And yet, it's not the end. Life happens, changes occur, and you'll want to integrate some changes into your trust, as we've discussed. Remember that an estate attorney, a financial advisor, and a tax expert work together for you as your estate planning pit crew—fine-tuning every part, so your plan performs exactly as intended.

Estate documents handle the 'how'. But your heart—the 'why'—often deserves its place in the plan. Legal language can't always capture emotional nuance. A legacy letter is a heartfelt message to your heirs that offers comfort, connection, and guidance that your loved ones will treasure. In that letter, it is best to share the meaning behind specific gifts or decisions and your hopes for how assets will be used; reflections on your values and life lessons; family stories, blessings, or expressions of gratitude.

Finalizing your estate plan lifts an invisible weight, not just from your own shoulders, but also from those who love you. This estate plan ensures your affairs are in order, fulfilling your wishes and eliminating worries.

For your loved ones, it means avoiding courtroom stress and unnecessary delays, and knowing what your intentions are now that all is said and done.

Remember that estate plans and their components are living documents. Revisit them as life evolves, adjust when needed, and continue conversations. Keep your plan—and your legacy—active and aligned. Your diligence creates freedom and peace later.

How a Living Trust Solves Real Problems

Case Study 1: Blended Family Inheritance Split

The Situation

Linda remarried in her early 60s after being widowed. She and her new spouse each had adult children from previous marriages. Linda wanted to ensure her husband was financially secure for life—but also that her children ultimately received their inheritance.

The Challenge

Without careful planning, assets could pass entirely to the surviving spouse, leaving children unintentionally disinherited.

The Trust Solution

Linda created a revocable living trust that allowed her spouse to use certain assets during his lifetime, while clearly directing that the remaining assets would pass to her children upon his death.

The Result

The trust protected both generations, honored Linda's wishes, and reduced the likelihood of family conflict or misunderstandings later.

Case Study 2: Business Succession Inside a Trust

The Situation

Mark owned a small family business that provided income for his household. One child was actively involved in the business, while the others were not.

The Challenge

Mark wanted the business to continue smoothly without disputes or forced sales after his death.

The Trust Solution

His living trust outlined exactly how the business would be managed, who would control operations, and how non-participating heirs would be compensated through other assets.

The Result

The trust provided continuity, protected the business, and prevented conflict between siblings over ownership and control.

Case Study 3: Caring for a Dependent With Disabilities

The Situation

Susan had an adult son with a disability who relied on government benefits and ongoing care.

The Challenge

An outright inheritance could jeopardize her son's eligibility for essential assistance.

The Trust Solution

Susan worked with an attorney to incorporate special needs planning into her trust, ensuring funds could be used to enhance her son's quality of life without disrupting benefits.

The Result

Her son remained protected, supported, and financially secure, with a trustee overseeing distributions according to Susan's instructions.

Case Study 4: Avoiding Family Disputes With Clear Trustee Powers

The Situation

After the family patriarch passed away, disagreements arose among the adult children about distributions, asset management, and timing.

The Challenge

Vague instructions and unclear trustee authority created tension and delayed resolutions.

The Trust Solution

A well-drafted living trust clearly defines trustee powers, timelines, and discretion, reducing ambiguity and limiting emotional decision-making.

The Result

The trustee could act confidently, disputes were minimized, and the family avoided costly legal battles.

Your Review Is Appreciated

Thank you! I hope you found this a helpful guide as you plan your future. If this book gave you clarity and confidence, your honest review is appreciated. It not only helps other families find the guidance they're looking for but also helps me keep creating practical resources. Scan the QR code below:

Conclusion

"The greatest purpose of life is to live it for something that will last longer than you." — ***William James***

Take a moment to acknowledge what you've learned and the new decisions you have made as you read this book. What began as a complex and intimidating topic—estate planning through living trusts—has hopefully revealed itself to be a clear and empowering path toward protecting what matters most. Hint: It's not the money!

Your loved ones, your values, and your legacy are encapsulated in your trust documents.

Living trusts are more than legal instruments; they are vessels of intention, allowing you to control the distribution of your financial legacy. They avoid the complications of probate, reduce tax burdens, and ensure your assets are transferred smoothly and privately. Beyond the practical benefits, living trusts offer something deeply human: the ability to plan with love and purpose.

From Knowledge to Action: Your 90-Day Road Map

The 90-Day Road Map at the beginning of this book was crafted to eliminate the guesswork involved in estate planning. Step by step, you have built the scaffolding of an estate plan that is legally sound and emotionally meaningful.

Go back into the 90-Day Roadmap now. Keep written lists and notes of which steps you have already taken, the next ones to take care of, and schedule the meetings with professionals in plenty of time. Yes, you can take the time to DIY your draft trust or will first. Why not? The software tools are out there if you're comfortable with the small learning curve involved.

Whether you begin with DIY in mind or go straight to an estate attorney as your first stop, keep refining the plan you've created. Be alert to any changes your trust documents, will, or powers of attorney require; make those amendments immediately—none of us knows what tomorrow will bring.

Be Proud:

- You didn't leave your wealth-building to chance
- You didn't leave your legacy to chance, either
- You documented your goals, wishes, and intentions with foresight, attention to detail, and care for the relationships

you’ve spent a lifetime nurturing.

For that, your future self—and your family—will thank you.

So move forward with confidence. Revisit what you’ve built when needed, and know that because of your effort, the people you love will one day experience the peace, clarity, and security that only purposeful planning can provide. *Your legacy is not just protected; it’s alive.*

Glossary of Terms

Amendment - A legal document that modifies specific sections of an existing trust while leaving the rest intact.

Asset Protection Trust - An irrevocable trust designed to shield assets from creditors, lawsuits, and legal claims.

Beneficiary - A person or organization designated to receive assets from a trust, will, or other estate planning document.

Bequest - A gift of property or assets left to someone through a will or trust.

Charitable Lead Trust (CLT) - An irrevocable trust that provides financial support to charities for a set term, then distributes remaining assets to non-charitable beneficiaries.

Charitable Remainder Trust (CRT) - A trust that pays income to the grantor or beneficiary for a set period, then transfers the remaining assets to charity.

Community Property - Property acquired during marriage that belongs equally to both spouses, recognized in certain states.

Conservatorship - A court-supervised arrangement where someone is appointed to manage another person's financial affairs due to incapacity.

Dynasty Trust - An irrevocable trust designed to pass wealth through multiple generations while minimizing estate taxes.

Estate Tax - A federal or state tax imposed on the total value of a deceased person's estate before distribution to heirs.

Fiduciary - A person legally obligated to act in another's best interest, such as a trustee managing trust assets.

Funding the Trust - The process of transferring ownership of assets into a trust's name.

Generation-Skipping Transfer Tax (GSTT) - A federal tax on transfers of assets that skip a generation, such as from grandparent to grandchild.

Grantor - The person who creates and funds a trust (also called settlor or trustor).

Grantor Retained Annuity Trust (GRAT) - A trust that allows the grantor to transfer appreciating assets to heirs with minimal gift tax exposure.

Guardian - A person appointed to care for minor children or manage their affairs.

Inheritance Tax - A tax paid by beneficiaries on assets they inherit, imposed by some states.

Intentionally Defective Grantor Trust (IDGT) - A trust structure that removes asset appreciation from the grantor's estate while the grantor pays income taxes.

Intestate - Dying without a valid will, causing assets to be distributed according to state law.

Irrevocable Life Insurance Trust (ILIT) - An irrevocable trust that owns life insurance policies to remove death benefits from the taxable estate.

Irrevocable Trust - A trust that cannot be easily modified or revoked once established, offering stronger asset protection and tax benefits.

Joint Tenancy with Rights of Survivorship - A form of property ownership where the surviving owner automatically inherits the deceased owner's share.

Living Trust - A trust created during the grantor's lifetime that can manage assets during incapacity and distribute them after death without probate.

Living Will - A document stating preferences for medical treatment if unable to communicate (also called advance directive).

Payable-on-Death (POD) - A beneficiary designation that allows assets to transfer directly to named beneficiaries without probate.

Pour-Over Will - A will designed to transfer any assets not already in a trust into the trust upon death.

Power of Attorney - A legal document authorizing someone to act on another's behalf for financial or healthcare decisions.

Probate - The court-supervised process of validating a will and distributing a deceased person's assets.

Qualified Personal Residence Trust (QPRT) - A trust that allows transfer of a residence to heirs at reduced gift tax value while retaining the right to live there.

Restatement - A complete rewrite of a trust document that replaces the original while maintaining the same creation date.

Revocable Trust - A trust that can be modified, amended, or revoked by the grantor during their lifetime.

Spendthrift Trust - A trust that protects beneficiaries from their own poor financial decisions by controlling distributions through a trustee.

Special Needs Trust - A trust designed to provide for disabled beneficiaries without affecting their government benefits.

Step-Up in Basis - A tax rule that adjusts the cost basis of inherited assets to their fair market value at death, potentially reducing capital gains taxes.

Successor Trustee - The person or institution named to take over trust management when the original trustee can no longer serve.

Tenancy by the Entirety - A form of joint ownership available to married couples that provides protection from individual creditors.

Transfer-on-Death (TOD) - A beneficiary designation allowing certain assets to pass directly to beneficiaries without probate.

Trust Protector - A person with limited powers to modify an irrevocable trust or replace trustees as circumstances change.

Trustee - The person or institution responsible for managing trust assets and carrying out the grantor's instructions.

Uniform Probate Code (UPC) - A standardized set of laws adopted by some states to simplify probate procedures.

Will (Last Will and Testament) - A legal document that directs how assets should be distributed after death, subject to probate court validation.

References

Artificial Intelligence (AI) and Trust and Estate Law. (2024, May 2). The American College of Trust and Estate Counsel. https://www.actec.org/resources-for-wealth-planning-professionals/artificial-intelligence-and-trust-and-estate-law-ai/

Benefits of Cloud Storage for Law Firms: Security, Accessibility, and Efficiency. (2024, September 18). Bloomfield Networks. https://www.bloomfieldnetworks.com/2024/09/18/benefits-of-cloud-storage/

Bruni, J. (2024, August 26). Building Trust Through Effective Data Security And Risk Management. *Forbes*. https://www.forbes.com/councils/forbesbusinesscouncil/2024/08/26/building-trust-through-effective-data-security-and-risk-management/

Charitable Remainder Trusts. (n.d.). Internal Revenue Service. https://www.irs.gov/charities-non-profits/charitable-remainder-trusts

Choosing the Right Trustee. (2024, May 9). Fiduciary Trust. https://www.fiduciary-trust.com/insights/choosing-the-right-trustee/

Damsgaard, M. (2024, January 31). *Offshore Asset Protection Trust Jurisdictions: Key Locations for Secure Wealth Protection*. Global Residence Index. https://globalresidenceindex.com/offshore-asset-protection-trusts/

Diehl, R., JD. (2024, March 5). *To Avoid Probate, Use Trusts for Estate Planning*. Kiplinger. https://www.kiplinger.com/retirement/to-avoid-probate-use-trusts-for-estate-planning

Dumm, C. W. (2025, January 10). How to Create a Living Trust. *Protecting Wealth*. https://protectingwealth.com/how-to-create-a-living-trust/

Emmer, R. (2023, September 12). *Intergenerational Communication in Legacy Wealth Management: Facilitating Family Conversations*. Silversage. https://robertemmer.com/intergenerational-communication-in-legacy-wealth-management/

Estate Beneficiary: What Is It and How to Choose One. (2025). Bank of America Private Bank. https://www.privatebank.bankofamerica.com/financial-education/estate-beneficiaries.html

Estate planning for digital assets. (n.d.). Fidelity. https://www.fidelity.com/viewpoints/wealth-management/estate-planning-for-digital-assets

Estate Tax. (2010). Internal Revenue Service. https://www.irs.gov/businesses/small-businesses-self-employed/estate-tax

Ettinger Law Firm. (2017, September 28). *Estate Planning and Identity Theft*. New York Estate Planning & Elder Law Blog. https://www.trustlaw.com/blog/estate-planning-identity-theft/

Finding an estate planning attorney. (2023, August 15). Fidelity. https://www.fidelity.com/viewpoints/wealth-management/finding-an-estate-planning-attorney

Gurgold, E. (2018, January 30). *The Importance of Properly Titling Assets for Estate Planning Purposes*. Henderson, Franklin, Starnes & Holt, P.A.; Henderson, Franklin, Starnes & Holt, P.A

. https://www.henlaw.com/news-insights/the-importance-of-properly-titling-assets-for-estate-planning-purposes/

Hartman, R., Stewart, T., & Marquardt, K. (2025). *The Best Online Will-Making Programs.* U.S. News & World Report. https://money.usnews.com/money/retirement/aging/articles/the-best-online-will-making-programs

How a Living Trust Impacts Your Taxes. (n.d.). Rocketlawyer .https://www.rocketlawyer.com/family-and-personal/estate-planning/set-up-a-trust/legal-guide/tax-consequences-of-a-living-trust

How a Living Trust Preserves Your Privacy. (2024, July 31). *Mykajabi.* https://law.mykajabi.com/blog/how-a-living-trust-preserves-your-privacy

Hubbert, J. (2017, March 27). When Should I Update My Living Trust—and How? *Law Offices of Graham & Hubbert.* https://www.hubbertlaw.com/blog/estate-planning/2017/03/when-should-i-update-my-living-trust/

IRS Changes Rules on Irrevocable Trusts: What It Means for Your Estate Plan. (2024, October 30). The Law Firm of Brown & Jensen. https://www.bncjlaw.com/posts/irs-changes-rules-on-irrevocable-trusts-what-it-means-for-your-estate-plan

Law, P. (2023, September 18). Managing Beneficiary Expectations and More in Surprise, Sun City West, Buckeye, Arizona. *Pennington Law, PLLC.* https://www.penningtonestateplanning.com/blog/managing-beneficiary-expectations/

Lawyer Licensing. (2025). Americanbar.org. https://www.americanbar.org/groups/legal_services/flh-home/flh-lawyer-licensing/

LexWorkplace. (2023, July 24). LexWorkplace. https://lexworkplace.com/practice-areas/estate-planning/

Living Trust - Create Living Trust Forms Online. (n.d.). LegalZoom. https://www.legalzoom.com/personal/estate-planning/living-trust-overview.html

Living Trust Form (Revocable). (2016). EForms. https://eforms.com/living-trust/

Living Trust vs. Will: Key Differences & Which to Choose. (2025). MetLife. https://www.metlife.com/stories/legal/living-trust-vs-will/

Livingston, T. (2024, September 18). *Understanding the True Cost of Estate Planning: A Comprehensive Guide for Every Budget*. BlueNotary. https://bluenotary.us/cost-of-estate-planning/

McCall, J. J. & Perotti, M. (n.d.). *Estate and Tax Planning 2023 Update: Act While You Can*. Pillsbury Law. https://www.pillsburylaw.com/en/news-and-insights/estate-tax-planning-2023-update.html

McDuffy, T. (2009, January 13). *How Probate Works: A State Comparison*. LegalMatch Law Library. https://www.legalmatch.com/law-library/article/how-probate-works-a-state-comparison.html

Morgan, J. P. (2024, November 18). *Communicating Your Estate Plan with Your Family*. J.P. Morgan. https://www.jpmorgan.com/insights/wealth-planning/trusts-and-estates/we-need-to-talk-communicating-your-estate-plan-with-your-family

N-Able. (2020, March 31). *11 Best Practices for Document Management Security*. (2020, March 31). N-Able. https://www.n-able.com/it/blog/11-best-practices-for-document-management-security

Preparing Heirs for the Responsibility of Wealth Management. (2025). Financialregulationcourses. https://www.financialregulationcourses.com/preparing-heirs-responsibility-wealth-management

Protecting Your Assets in Trusts and LLCs (2023, March 7). USI. https://www.usi.com/executive-insights/executive-series-articles/featured/personal-risk/q1-2023/protecting-your-assets-in-trusts-and-llcs/

Segal, T. (2024, Oct 31). *Questions to Ask Your Estate-Planning Attorney*. Investopedia. https://www.investopedia.com/articles/personal-finance/070815/10-questions-ask-your-estate-planning-attorney.asp

Sember, B. (2015, June 22). *How to change a living trust*. LegalZoom. https://www.legalzoom.com/articles/how-to-change-a-living-trust

Semczuk, N. (2023, December 12). *Revocable Trust Vs. Irrevocable Trust: Key Differences*. Bankrate. https://www.bankrate.com/investing/revocable-trust-vs-irrevocable-trust/

Seven Common Living Trust Mistakes and How to Avoid Them. (2024, July 17). Law Office of Jonathan D. Alexander, Esq. https://www.orangecountyestateplanningattorney.com/blog/seven-common-living-trust-mistakes-and-how-to-avoid-them/

Simpson, D. W. (2024, July 17). *Build Your Legacy and Leave a Lasting Impact*. DW Simpson. https://www.dwsimpson.com/2024/07/17/build-your-legacy-and-leave-a-lasting-impact/

10 Tips to Avoid Probate. (n.d.). Legal Zoom. https://www.legalzoom.com/articles/10-tips-to-avoid-probate

Tax benefits of trusts. (n.d.). Empathy. https://www.empathy.com/taxes/tax-benefits-of-trusts

TLG Web Admin. (2024, July 23). *Changing Beneficiaries of a Trust: Essential Steps & Legal Insights*. Stevenson Law Office. https://stevensonlawoffice.com/updating-trust-beneficiaries-legal-guides-best-practices/

Trust Protectors Explained. (2023, October 27). Bressler.com. https://www.bressler.com/publication-trust-protectors-explained

Trusts & Estates 50-State Charts Toolkit | Practical Law. (2025). Westlaw. https://content.next.westlaw.com/practical-law/document/Ibe7995a35c0511e79bef99c0ee06c731/Trusts-Estates-50-State-Charts-Toolkit?viewType=FullText&transitionType=Default&contextData=(sc.Default)

Understanding trusts. (n.d.). Bank of America Private Bank. https://www.privatebank.bankofamerica.com/financial-education/understanding-trusts.html

Varga, L. (2024, November 13). *How to Set Up a Living Trust in California: A Step-by-Step Guide*. Moravec Varga & Mooney. https://www.moravecslaw.com/post/how-to-set-up-a-living-trust-in-california-a-step-by-step-guide

What's the Difference Between Estate Tax & Inheritance Tax? (2019, December 17). Western & Southern Financial Group. https://www.westernsouthern.com/retirement/estate-tax-vs-inheritance-tax

Yushkov, A. (2023, October 10). *Does Your State Have an Estate or Inheritance Tax?* Tax Foundation. https://taxfoundation.org/data/all/state/state-estate-tax-inheritance-tax-2023/

Made in the USA
Monee, IL
14 September 2026

62974505R00111